# ELECTRIC YOUNG WRITERS' ANTHOLOGY 2015

First edition

This book is a work of fiction. Names, characters, businesses, organisatons, places, events, and incidents are the product either of the author's imagination or are used fictitiously. Any resemblance to actual persons, living or dead, events, or locales is entirely coincidental.

Copyright © Electric Reads 2015

The right of Electric Reads to be identified as copyright owner of this work has been asserted by them in accordance with the Copyright, Designs and Patents Act 1998.

All rights reserved. Published in the United Kingdom by Electric Reads, London.

www.electricreads.com

ISBN (paperback): 978-0-9931305-6-4
ISBN (e-book, kindle): 978-0-9931305-8-8

Thanks to Stephen, Chandrashekhar, Vanessa, Dragan, Rajendra, and Lizzie for their help in preparing the anthology for publication.

All rights reserved. Apart from any use under UK copyright law no part of this publication may be reproduced, stored in a retrieval system, or transmitted, in any form or by any means, without prior written permission of the publisher, nor be otherwise circulated in any form of binding or cover other than that in which it is published and without a similar condition being imposed on the subsequent publisher.

10 9 8 7 6 5 4 3 2 1

# YOUNG WRITERS' ANTHOLOGY 2015

ELECTRIC READS

# CONTENTS

FOREWORD ............................................................................................. VII
CYRINE SINTI: Courtesan Cartel ............................................................... 1
BETH GADSBY: Where The Forgotten Things Go. ..................................... 11
HANNAH MICKLEBURGH: Now I Will Believe That There Are Unicorns ..... 27
STEPHANIE GALLON: Dotty Grim And The Red-Hooded Herring ............. 35
HARRY DRAPER: Last Time ...................................................................... 41
LEXY HUDSON: Well Versed ..................................................................... 47
CJS WILLIAMS: Measured In Coffee Spoons ........................................... 57
JESSICA TREMLETT: Soup ....................................................................... 67
IRAM AHMED: The Cores ......................................................................... 77
SÎAN ROWE: The Butterfly Theory ........................................................... 87
MELISSA WELLIVER: The War Letters ..................................................... 93
KATIE LUMSDEN: Threads ....................................................................... 107
FIONA MCCORMACK: Mona Lisa ............................................................. 117
EOIN WEST: Deep Space .......................................................................... 125
ANIKA RAJDEV: The Evolution ................................................................. 135
BRYONY PORTEOUS-SEBOUHIAN: The Drude. ....................................... 145
CHRISTIAN ROBSHAW: The End Is The Middle ....................................... 157
HANNAH M KING: The Dorstan Fall .......................................................... 163
MEGAN ATKINS: Temporal Tracers .......................................................... 173
DAVID KRAJNYAK: Censorship ................................................................ 189
ELLIE PAYNE: Lesser Of Two Evils ........................................................... 195
ANDREW HEALEY: Freshwater Lover ...................................................... 207
CHRISTINA FOSTER: Not A Fairy Tale ...................................................... 213
MATTHEW WILCOX: Strings ..................................................................... 223
HARRIET AVERY: Isla ................................................................................ 233

# FOREWORD
## MATTHEW SELWYN

Matthew Selwyn is a young writer from London, England. His debut novel, \*\*\*\*: *or, The Anatomy of Melancholy* was released in 2014. A student and librarian, he is often to be found hiding amongst the stacks in the Victorian library where he works, surrounded by piles of books. He writes book reviews online at www.bibliofreak.net.

Writing is important. The internet may be leading us into an increasingly visual world but underpinning everything we do are the stories that help us understand our reality. Without language, without narrative, life is a shapeless sludge. Words are the building blocks of what make us human and ever since we crawled out of the primordial goop that we didn't call 'home' we've developed increasingly sophisticated ways of expressing ourselves through language. This versatile, ever-evolving feast is humanity's greatest invention. That, or the man-bun – it's too early to say.

If language is humanity's greatest invention then it is writers who are custodians to our greatest gift. Without coming over all Shelleyan, writers are important to any society worth living in (sorry, Plato). They may not cure illnesses, feed or clothe us; I'm pretty sure Maslow's hierarchy of needs doesn't include poetry on any of the basic levels. And yet humans are more than biological automatons, going about life simply existing. Writing, art more generally, is what makes the hours spent filling in your tax return, sitting in your doctors' waiting room, listening to Gavin from accounts tell you about his week, worth living through. Without art, existence is just that.

It is often said that you should judge a society by how well it treats its weakest members. If that is a measure of a society's moral compass then I would suggest that how well it nurtures its young artists is a measure of its soul. That the arts are being increasingly impoverished in Britain as funding is moved elsewhere or removed altogether, is a sad indictment of a society who is blinded by the measurable and ignores the transcendent. As custodians of humanity's greatest gift, writers should be cherished and given room to grow and develop. An anthology like this one is an invaluable opportunity for twenty-five young writers to showcase their talent and grasp at the bottom rung of the ladder that leads to literary superstardom.

Okay, the days of literary superstardom are long gone – anything above indifference from the wider public is probably as high as any burgeoning literary talent has a right to aim. That, however, is very much the point: while Shelley was declaring that poets were legislators of the world (even the ones who didn't write poetry), literary superstardom was a real possibility. If comedy is the new rock and roll then Russell Brand is the new Jagger who was, skip a few, the new Byron. Sadly, few of today's writers sport bejewelled getups and strut around Europe causing all sorts of bother. In fact, few writers can even be defined solely as writers. Most are part-timers, who work other jobs while fitting in their creative output around the daily grind. It's hardly a lifestyle conducive to the creation of great art.

Almost a century ago, Virginia Woolf wrote that all a woman needed to write was five hundred pounds a year and a room of one's own. Not much has changed (except for what five hundred pounds buys you). With the explosion of self-publishing it has never been easier for an aspiring writer to gain the legitimacy of being able to call themselves a 'published' author. Yet at the same time, it has never been easier for a writer's voice to be lost among the cacophony of noise in digital space. What a young writer needs is no longer just time and space but an audience, an informed audience.

Having an opportunity to present their work in a collection such as this one is no small thing for a new writer. To have their work edited and buffed up to be its best and then to have it published in a form that encourages readers to dip into something new is a fantastic opportunity. Amongst the pages of this anthology are some future stars of literature – their pieces fuse great ideas with different styles of writing. One of the best things about this project, set up by Electric Reads, is that every genre of fiction is treated equally. Each writer has the complete freedom to write in a style and a genre that suits them and explore what interests them. This is a freedom that few writers receive and it is fantastic to see talented young writers flexing their creative muscles and letting it all hang out on the page.

I hope sincerely that projects like this one will help encourage new writers to pursue their creative endeavours with as much freedom as possible and that society will begin to once more appreciate and support the arts for what they are: the thing that gives life shape and colour.

# CYRINE SINTI
## COURTESAN CARTEL

Cyrine Sinti is a twenty-three-year-old writer and Bellydancer. Recently graduated, Cyrine has won two awards for her writing and she is working on a semi-fictional account of her childhood in an Eastern European Gypsy ghetto. An avid dancer, she also enjoys costume making, Burlesque, Wrestling and Circus performing. She has plans to create her own travelling Circus alongside writing.

*India 1951*

I was only 14 when she sold me. I wasn't anything special to look at but I was light skinned and tight, so I was instantly irresistible to the waves of hungry men that passed through Chingaari. Growing up together in the brothel we were like sisters. Rakhi was older than me by twelve years but we were inseparable. Whilst our mothers were working, Rakhi was raising me. She taught me how to dance, sew, walk with my bottom swaying and how to put on our 'high society' voices in case an Englishman wanted to whisk us away.

My Ama, my mother, always said that Rakhi's heart was too good for a place like Chingaari and I agreed with her. She was always doing my chores for me, letting me have naps during the day when everyone else was busy with their own work. She'd cut her own bathtimes in half so that I could have longer in the warm water. She'd rub oil into my hair until I fell asleep. She'd wake up earlier than me to go to the market and get me fresh juice in flasks so that I wouldn't have to endure Latifa's brown, watery tea with bits of cardamom floating around.

Latifa wasn't much of a cook but it was the only work available to the ageing dancer. She used to work as a Kathak dancer in a brothel in Bombay but after a run in with an angry wife and hot mustard oil, she had taken to working in the kitchens at Chingaari so as to hide her scarred face. Rakhi used to scold us if we made fun of Latifa; she'd tell us how bad Latifa must feel, *'having to hide from the men who once used to throw a month's wages at your beauty just because they can't stomach your bubbled face.'*

That's what Chingaari was: a palatial mansion to hide, away from the stiff, sareed women with their judging scowls and their oiled husbands pretending they didn't salivate like dogs at even the mention of the rose coloured gates of Chingaari. A haven for the washed up, the disfigured, the transsexuals, the homosexuals, the very-sexuals and a place for those who the *very* respectable men of India decided had no place in their *very* respectable India.

Every so often a young girl who had been disowned by her family for something as shameful as baring her shoulders would come knocking on the gates. She'd be let in and given a bed for a night and before long she'd be working in the bedrooms herself. Many of the girls ended up overdosing on opium or being beaten to death by one of their clients. But there were also a handful of girls who grew to love what they did.

Diljaan was one of those girls. She had the bed next to mine so I was often regaled with tales of what new and exciting things she had discovered with her clients. She would lean forward and let one of her deep brown legs hang over the side of her bed, "Mathi *mulethi*" I had got the nickname of *mulethi*, liquorice, from Diljaan because I had skinny, hard arms that looked like the rolls of liquorice root that Latifa kept tied in rags near her bed. "Mathi, I can't tell you how it feels to know that there are men out there who are so in love with me that they break their *phere,* their vows, taken in God's own house, just to pay for the privilege of having me for half an hour" She leaned back with a flourish of her hand, - lifted her leg in the air and began shaking her anklets.

She fascinated me from a young age as she made her work look glamourous and fun. She'd take longer than everyone else getting ready. She'd do her hair in elaborate plaits with flowers and mint leaves tucked into every cross. The mint leaves were for her to chew on in case she had to have anything unsavoury in her mouth. She would paint her face vibrant colours and use kohl around her eyes as if she were dancing for a Mughal court.

She'd speed through her chores quicker than the other girls so that she could practise her mujra dances. Latifa loved Diljaan the most because Diljaan would constantly pick her brains over her Kathak dancing. They would practice together in the morning whilst everyone was eating breakfast, sometimes I would sneak outside to watch them by the fountain dancing silently as the sun bathed them in a regal glow. Like sheets against the sun they whirled and dipped.

From little shy me to the alluring, poised Diljaan, Chingaari had open gates for everyone. All we had to do was pledge allegiance to our Memsahib, our 'Madame', Zoraida.

She was the owner of Chingaari and all that lived inside. From the highest-paid dancers to the flies that hovered over our sweet milk-tea, everything belonged to her. Our mothers never saw the money they lay under hordes of men for. Everything went to Zoraida- (or Ma Malik, Mother Boss, as the women called her). If any of the women needed to buy anything, they'd spend days pacing nervously around our room agonizing over the best time to approach Ma Malik. We all shared a huge room in the basement of Chingaari, there were rows of box-rooms on the upper floors that were reserved for 'work hours' only. We weren't allowed to live in them, we had our room buried under Chingaari. Beds lined the walls with flowers wrapped around the edge, makeshift mosquito nets made of old saree fabric draped over and sticks of incense shoved in the cracks of the wall.

Incense was everywhere in Chingaari. Placed on the peach coloured walls that wrapped up the huge palace-like building- making it look like a temple to those who were new to the area. I suppose in some ways, it was a temple. Desperate men came and worshiped shiny clothed figures. Then the men would reach their personal enlightenment after an hour in the small, cell-like bedrooms.

It was a beautiful looking building from afar- the windows were framed with carved images from the Kamasutra, embedded in what looked like gold-plate. In actuality, it was just wood painted dark yellow. That's what we relied on for trade - illusions. The cracks in the fountain looked like marble from a distance. The building looked as if it was mysteriously swathed in shadows but upon entering you could see the dirty streaks on the pale pink exterior. I once asked Ama why, with all the money Ma Malik had spent on the inside of the house, she wouldn't clean up the outside. Her response was "When the men first see Chingaari, they see a shadowed palace with a grand marble fountain and windows fit for the Taj Mahal. By the time they get closer and see the truth, they're too drunk and set on passion to care. The reason no expense is spared for the inside is because we are the same as the outside" I looked at her confused, "Mathi, we aren't all filmi stars like Nargis or Madhubala. We are women who spend all day being basted by our sweat and dirt in the sun and all night being bathed in the sweat and juices of whoever has brought us for that moment. As long as everything else is sparkling, they won't notice that we are a little flat"

A stranger would say that it was sweet of Ma Malik to make sure that the women's flaws were hidden and veiled by the grandness of Chingaari's interior. But something about Ma Malik terrified all of us. Even the moths and flies never seemed to bother her. She appeared immortal and invincible, sat on the highest balcony of Chingaari, with her personal maid Jamila fanning her, whilst looking down at us squabbling over the flimsy flatbreads and watery lentils that Latifa had struggled out. She made us so much more aware of our mortality when she did this. With the sun enveloping her head and casting shadows over her body, she truly looked Godlike gazing down at us.

More than once I had heard Rakhi breathlessly wish for "Just a place at her feet." She thought nobody could hear her, but I could. I always heard her wish for the same thing whenever Ma Malik blessed us with her face. Rakhi's eyes would go wide and then narrow, she'd have the type of face my Ama did when she'd been using Latifa's hookah in the kitchen, she'd shake her head so slightly and then say the same thing "All I want is a place at her feet". Nobody loved Ma Malik more than Rakhi I think.

Rakhi always used to scold me whenever I spoke of Ma Malik. She'd tell me that I was better than Chingaari, that I could use my embroidery skills and be a seamstress for all the old high-society wives who smelt of mustard oil and looked at their husbands with disgust and then winked at their young Tonga drivers. I would've loved that life. I still long for it. I would love to have my own room with some of my decorated pillow-covers pinned to the door frame so people can look at the peacocks and flowers I'd stitched and see how good I am. I could even pay one of the beggar children to bring fresh juice to my clients, free of course. Rakhi's eyes held so much life and happiness that it made me believe every word she said. She saw my future through her dilated pupils when she'd gush over my latest completed embroidery work. She'd give me piles of bangles just to embroider the edge of her scarves so that she could pretend she was Madhubala with her own private seamstress.

I used to include her in my daydreams, thinking of her as my own personal dress-up doll. With her long, oiled hair, her soft brown eyes and the scar she had hidden in her eyebrows- (caused when she ran into Latifa's fist after stealing some sugar cane for me when I was younger). Rakhi seemed happy to stay at Chingaari; unlike the other girls, she never spoke about leaving. In my heart I knew that all she wanted was to be like Jamila. To be with Ma Malik every day. For her Ma Malik was her God, her bread and her breath. Ma Malik never got Rakhi's name right but it never bothered her. Just her presence was enough to keep Rakhi alive and happy. I realised this the spring before the accident.

Ma Malik was riding into town to collect rent from families who she had stuffed into crumbling rooms for extortionate prices. Rakhi had been awake since dawn scrubbing the driveway and gates and picking out the leaves from the cracked fountain in front of our building. Ma Malik came gliding out, her eyes never seemed to look at the floor. She just looked onwards. Rakhi was trailing behind her like a frayed thread.

"I will watch the roads for your return Ma!" Rakhi looked as shocked as the rest of us that she had spoken in the presence of Ma Malik without being told to. Everyone was quiet. I could see Jamila's hand twitching about to reach for the small strip of leather she kept tucked into the waistline of her saree. But Ma Malik held out her hand and turned to face Rakhi. I could hear a few hushed murmurs as some of the women began to pray for Rakhi.

"Rekha, the roads are for the rats and the piss of the street-children, if you want to watch for me then you raise your head higher. *Hum suraj banke aaungi*, I will return as the sun." She turned and carried on out of the gates- leaving Rakhi breathing heavily and swaying on the spot, her eyes fixed to the sky.

My Ama always says that it was that afternoon that Rakhi began to lose her mind.

I always say that Rakhi's mind was gone long before that.

Long before that afternoon where she sat and watched the sun for hours and had to wear ice cold scraps of fabric tied to her eyes for the week after. Long before that afternoon where she afterwards demanded to be called Rekha until the next time Ma Malik got her name wrong.

I think her mind was always gone when it came to Ma Malik. Rakhi's own Ama was what people thought of when they heard the word 'Kohtewali', 'Courtesan'. A tobacco-chewing, bruise and sore addled, opium-huffing, unwashed disgrace named Meera. Because of this I think Rakhi was naturally drawn to Ma Malik as a mother figure because she was such a stark contrast to Meera.

Luckily for me, my Ama wasn't born into the prostitute life as Meera was. My Ama's parents were killed when they were travelling to Uttar Pradesh and eventually Ama ended up here after her uncles took in her brothers but not her.

Not that it mattered to anyone outside Chingaari. To them we were all dirty, sex-starved witches who had no right living whilst so many were dying, starved in the unforgiving heat of India. Women hated us because we took their men from them and returned them drunk, diseased and penniless and men hated us because they were unable to stop themselves.

Even now at twenty-five years of age, I cannot understand what was so addicting about us. We were tempting, I understand this. The smell of incense and freshly ground herbs and spices infused with the air and created the aroma of comfort and love. The love that the proper wives of high society men wouldn't *dare* lower themselves to perform. One could say that Chingaari smelt of immorality and those weak-willed men were high on the smell of shameless sin.

I can understand wanting to come inside Chingaari for the first time because it is such a commanding presence and the music and laughter can be heard on the balmy winds for miles. But visiting again and again just to spend time with women who can never offer you anything but their bodies and a bored moan here or there, choosing to leave your wife who knows your work schedule, doctors' appointments and favourite foods, to sleep in the stained beds of women who only know how much you could spend is madness to me.

This is why as I tell you this, I want you to understand that what happened is really nobody's fault. If there has to be blame then blame the ones who came night after night and threw their children's food and rent at our calloused feet. Blame the impossible rules for females that saw so many of them knocking on our gates for shelter. Blame the Indian tradition that has destroyed the lives of so many girls; men can spend all night in a brothel but wash themselves and become pure again whereas women must be beaten and shunned for daring to show their God-given flesh. Don't blame desperate people for doing desperate things.

You could even blame me. I was always so scared of everything. The few times I had shown courage was pointless, I ended up weeping, urinating or beaten. I should have seen what Rakhi was becoming. If I had maybe so much blood wouldn't have washed over Sonagacchi, stained the floors of Chingaari and sent a good, sweet girl into a power-crazed monster with eyes as dead as the one she had once almost blinded herself for.

~o~

As I am Romani Gypsy, I have always had an interest in India due to the similarities in our cultures. Through my dancing I have had the opportunity to travel throughout India and see many of the historical landmarks such as the Taj Mahal and the Golden Temple.

This grandeur and the richness of Indian culture gave me the idea of writing a novel about India as there is a wealth of inspiration in the architecture, music, fashion and even food. Visiting Sonagachi, Kolkata, the largest red light district in Asia, inspired me to write a 'gangster Bollywood-esque' novel about prostitution. Contrasting the high extravagance of Bollywood style settings with the seedy ruthlessness of the brothels is something I particularly enjoyed when planning out *Courtesan Cartel* and I particularly liked creating a world that showed women as both the victims as well as the perpetrators of the sex industry. I used a lot of research into 1950s Indian culture for the novel as well as situations I observed during my stay at Sonagachi.

'Once Upon a time in a land far away' is a line that is extremely appropriate to describe my reading and writing tastes. I've always enjoyed cultural novels such as Khaled Hosseini - *The Kite Runner* and Candy Miller – *Salt And Honey*. Reading and learning about a range of cultures and countries is one of my passions that is reflected in my own work. I adore the world and everyone in it so for me, this is the greatest way to know more about the opulent mix of nations and backgrounds.

I tie in my travels with my writing as I am always inspired by different countries and cultures. Whenever I get an idea for a novel, I prefer to visit the place and do first-hand exploration before I begin writing. I would like to introduce more of Romani culture into the mainstream via my writing.

# BETH GADSBY
## WHERE THE FORGOTTEN THINGS GO

Beth Gadsby, originally from Chesterfield in Derbyshire, is nineteen years old and is reading Linguistics with German at Newcastle University. She spends her free time working on a fantasy novel and helping to run her university's Creative Writing Society. She has previously been published in *The Red House Young Writers' Yearbook 2012*.

When the pain fades away, I wake to find I have been reborn at 51.5075 degrees north and -0.1279 degrees west – the place the humans of this time call London. The sun is halfway between the eastern horizon and the peak of the sky: for all of my kind, this reality will be a life of perpetual mornings.

It is 1824AD and it smells quite strongly of polished wood and oil paint. The humans in this building have adorned themselves either in floor-length dresses with puffy sleeves or long coats over waistcoats with frills at the neck. They talk quietly, gathering in twos and threes in front of coloured squares and rectangles hanging on the walls. This, then, must be an art gallery. I've been told humans find these 'paintings' beautiful. How peculiar of them, to find such meaning in appearances.

It is now, having surveyed my surroundings, that I realise: I am – we are – still on Earth. No Land Of The Forgotten for my kind – not yet. Not in this life. I sigh in relief.

But if not in this life, then perhaps the next. I am not about to let that happen. It's a good thing, then, that I like humans, otherwise I'd find preventing our fate rather dull.

The human I choose stands alone, staring at one of the paintings without moving. It doesn't even seem to be breathing. I'm told that's a bad thing. I go to stand next to it and, to my surprise, it senses my presence before I speak.

"Isn't it marvellous," it says to me in English, its voice deep and its tone assured, "that Claude created such depth and detail in this painting, and yet, would you believe, this seaport does not exist in actuality."

I squint at the rectangle on the wall, trying to see the *depth* and *detail* in the smudges of dull colour. "Simply marvellous," I agree nonetheless.

"Would it not be spectacular to have such an imagination as to…"

I glance at it when it trails off and find it looking at me – or rather, through me. Its face contorts, and it turns in a circle as if searching for something. "Where have you gone?"

"I haven't gone anywhere," I say. It jumps at the sound of my voice, and jumps even more when it feels my presence touch it. "I'm right here."

Its skin turns alarmingly pale. "I'm going mad," it mutters. Those words bring to mind the stabbing, sickening feeling of being walked through. I know the routine well enough by now: first comes the denial, then the disbelief. Then you might as well give up.

"No, no, you're not – my name's Anax and I'm what you'd call a time spirit. I'm not a ghost and I'm not trying to scare you and I promise you I'm very real – I'm as real as you are, believe me. Please believe me."

Its normal colour has not returned, but on the other hand, it hasn't run away either.

"*Please* believe me," I repeat, unable to think of any other way to convince it of my existence.

"This… This has got to be some kind of practical joke."

"It isn't, I swear it!" I reach out and touch it again. To my relief, my hand does not go through its arm, the way it would with a human that does not believe. "See? I'm right here. I'm real."

Now it really isn't breathing. I point this out; it takes a few pointedly deep breaths, clears its throat and readjusts its hat. Its voice is shaky when it speaks.

"What – ah – what did you say you were?"

"A time spirit." In the realities in which humans and time spirits understood each other and communicated freely, it was the humans that gave us this name, or so I am told by those who remember those realities.

"A… A what?"

I start to explain reincarnating into different realities, ageing through space and travelling through time – which humans tend to find as confusing as I find the notion of travelling north and south – but the human puts a hand to its face (which is still too pale) and shakes its head.

"I… I do apologise, but this is an awful lot to take in, you must understand." It goes and sits on one of the benches facing the paintings. It watches the ceiling quite intently for a few moments. Then it says, "What – what did you say your name was again?"

"Anax."

It nods. "Anax. How do you do, Anax." It shakes its head and – oddly – laughs. "I can't quite believe I'm conversing with a ghost."

"Time spirit," I correct. "Not ghost."

"Yes, of course." It sighs and shakes its head again.

"Do you have a name?" I ask, hoping to distract it from its shock.

"Yes," it murmurs. Then: "I mean, my name is Frederick Morris. How do you do?"

"How do I -? I, um, I do well. Thank you."

Frederick Morris looks at me, drawing its eyebrows close together, but flinches again when its eyes find no visible form.

Meanwhile, my line of latitude is moving beneath me, as it has been throughout the conversation, and I know I cannot stay here much longer.

"I'm going to have to go," I say.

Frederick Morris gasps. "Wait – but we've only just begun the conversation! I was hoping you'd at least be able to enlighten me on these – on these time spirits."

I will not have chance to explain before I leave this art gallery and Frederick Morris behind.

"Be on latitude 51.5075 degrees north, on Holland's eastern border, at dawn on the 29th of September of this year, and I'll explain then."

"Why not now?"

"I can't stay here; that's not how ageing through space works."

It sounds alarmed. "Ageing through space?"

I repeat the date, time and place I told it before, but before I can check that it has remembered them, the world has turned on its axis enough to put one of the art gallery's walls between us, and my new life begins.

I skip through time like small humans through a meadow. 725AD. 6501BC. 4237AD. Sometimes I stay in one time for miles and miles. Sometimes I change it every couple of metres. Always, the sun lingers halfway up the sky. A life of perpetual mornings.

It is 1933AD and I am over 3,500 miles old when I get a sudden whiff of wet fur.

"So you're still obsessed with humans, I take it," a lilting voice near me says in the mother tongue of the time spirits.

If I didn't recognise the voice, I'd know who's talking by the smell. My sibling Ral's presence – and smell – lingers close by to my right. It's been many lives since our lines of latitude came this close.

"Still hanging round too many dogs, I assume," I reply.

Ral's laugh is a barking one. "What can I say? They're fluffy. And they actually notice us. Seriously, Anax, what *do* you find so intriguing about creatures that are not fluffy and ignore you ninety percent of the time?"

I stare out at the scene in front of us: an open field where a group of humans are running around and throwing a single ball between them, laughing and shouting. Every so often, they come to a stop, and when one of them throws the ball, another hits it with a bat. I'm not sure what the point of it is.

"They fascinate me," I tell Ral. "What are they doing? Why are they doing it?"

Ral snorts. "Pointless question, if you ask me." We watch the humans for a few metres in silence. It does not make their movements make any more sense.

I draw breath to speak, then hesitate, knowing how Ral will respond, then decide to say it anyway.

"Besides, if humans don't believe in us, we'll be forgotten."

Ral scoffs. "When the elders say it, I just think they've experienced so many realities they're bound to be losing their touch. When *you* say it... Really, Anax? *Really?*"

"They have more mental power than you give them credit for," I argue. "How else do you explain the disappearance of dragons?"

Ral splutters before they manage to reply, sounding outraged. "Anax, listen to yourself! It doesn't make any sense, not in real life! Real humans can't communicate well enough to cause that sort of thing! The Land of the Forgotten is a *fairy story* the elders *made up* for new time spirits!"

"Clearly you've managed to miss quite a few serious discussions, then."

On the field in front of us, one of the humans hits the ball hard enough for it to come flying in our direction; I have to flit a few seconds into the future to avoid it hitting me. Ral follows suit to continue our conversation. One of the humans approaches to fetch the ball.

"Wait, hold on a metre – you're telling me that the elders *actually* think we're going to end up in the Land of the Forgotten with the dragons and the fairies if the humans stop believing in us?" Ral laughs harshly before I can even answer. At the sound of Ral's laughter, the human fetching the ball looks up at us.

"Is someone there?" it says in English, a twang in its voice giving it away as American.

"Only us," I reply. The human freezes. I nudge the ball in its direction but it does not move to retrieve it. Ral mutters something heatedly.

"Are you a ghost?" it says.

I sigh. Another human runs over before I can reply.

"Hey, are you alright?" the second human asks, patting the first on the back.

"I, uh, I think this place might be haunted," the first human says.

"Actually-" I begin, but the second human interrupts me:

"Come on, now, there's no such thing as ghosts. There's nothing there." It picks up the ball and the two of them set off back towards the rest of the group – and walk straight through us. Ral and I gasp and gag; being walked through pulls all the air out of you. It's a sickening experience.

The two humans notice nothing.

Ral chokes on their words as they draw my attention back to them, their voice raised and incredulous. "Anax, *what* was *that?*"

"Human language," I reply. "Or, one of the many human languages."

Ral splutters sounds which I'm sure are meant to be words but are completely unintelligible. Finally, they manage: "Alright, that's it. I've had quite enough of you and your humans and your nonsense. *Human language* indeed."

Ral does not wait for me to reply before their presence by my side disappears.

In only my first few realities were humans and time spirits allies, so I remember very little of them. One thing I do remember, oddly, is that humans often suffer from arthritis – probably because I have always wondered, towards the end of every life, if this is what it would feel like.

I have to go to September 1824AD long before I reach Holland to meet Frederick Morris: I know I will not have enough energy left to time travel when I reach that point. I hate staying in one time for too long. It's so restrictive. I don't understand how humans don't get bored to tears before they're fully grown.

I almost don't expect the human from the art gallery to meet me, but it does. As it did before, it feels my presence and greets me first.

"Anax?"

"Good morning, Frederick Morris."

Its laugh is shaky. "I must admit, I'm unsure whether to be relieved or terrified to find that you are indeed real. I had feared I had made you up and had made this journey in vain."

"You shouldn't doubt yourself so."

"It's easy to say that now," Frederick Morris says with a sigh.

It still flinches when I reach out to touch it. "You might want to hold on to me," I explain. "Time spirit ageing is rather fast and I don't want to leave you behind. What I do want you to do is to listen to what I tell you, and to tell your friends and your family about me and my kind, and get them to tell everyone they know. Convince them of the truth."

Frederick Morris's face contorts, but its hand closes firmly around my wrist, in the same way mine is clasped around its. "Why do you ask this of me?"

"Because nobody seems to believe in us anymore, which in my opinion is quite a problem."

"I suppose it must be terribly disheartening, to have no-one believe in one."

I sigh. "If only that were the only problem. You see…" I pause, trying to figure out the best way to explain it. "Human belief is a very powerful thing. If all humans stop believing in something from one reality to the next, it gets forgotten – by which I mean it completely disappears from this world. They must go *some*where, we think – a Land of the Forgotten, we call it. Some of us think it's just a story, but if that's so, then where *do* the forgotten things go?"

Frederick Morris looks at me with its mouth hanging open a little. I note with some small satisfaction that its gaze, following the direction of my voice, is unwavering.

"You worry that the time spirits will end up in the Land of the Forgotten," it says with a note of sadness in its voice.

"I do. One thing I've noticed about this reality is that less humans believe in us than in previous realities. In the first realities I experienced, all humans believed in us. I have experienced hundreds of realities since then. In this life, you are the only human I have truly been able to engage."

Frederick Morris speaks slowly. "What, exactly, do you mean by 'realities'?"

"Each time the time spirits are reborn, we see a different version of reality, each as true as the last. Sometimes only minor details change. Sometimes everything is entirely different."

"I see," Frederick Morris says, though it sounds dubious. It is no longer looking at me; it has been distracted by our surroundings. The horizons shift around us but the pale morning sunlight does not change. "Anax… How are we moving when we are standing still?"

"You know that humans move through space, and age through time," I begin. "For us, it's simply the other way around."

It focusses its attention on me again. "Why, that's nonsense! How can that possibly work?"

I chuckle. "Your way of doing things doesn't make much sense to me, either." Frederick Morris shakes its head, so I decide to elaborate. "We're all reborn – or, in some cases, born – on one line of longitude simultaneously. As the earth turns, we stay still in space and move through time, and we age along our respective lines of latitude. We die on the same line of longitude we are born on."

Frederick Morris sighs and rubs at its forehead with the hand not gripping my wrist.

"I can't quite believe this is happening," it mumbles.

That has the panic rising inside me. "No – Frederick Morris – it *is* happening, please believe –"

It throws its head back and laughs. It's a free, light-hearted sort of sound. "Firstly, it is not necessary to call me by *both* of my names. I don't suppose time spirits are so bothered about formalities as humans are, so you may simply call me Frederick. Secondly," it continues, reaching out for me with its free hand and holding on, "I have no doubts about your existence, Anax. I will always believe in you, and that's a promise."

"What about that one by the wall, on its own?"

Frederick has travelled with me since we met up a hundred miles or so ago. I enjoy its company (it plays the most delightful violin) and its presence makes any human we encounter much more likely to believe in my existence. These two things are enough to considerably lift my mood, despite the pain and the lack of energy that this place in life brings. I do not think I have ever been so upbeat having seen so many miles.

"Its?" Frederick repeats, its voice rising. "*Its?*"

I consider the word, confused. "What else would you have me call it?"

"She!" Frederick exclaims, as if it's obvious. "Her, on *her* own! She's a woman, not a – an *animal!*"

"I'm sorry. I did not mean to cause offence." Now that it (she?) mentions it, I do recall something about human pronouns from my earliest memories of my earliest lives. "So I should refer to humans with the pronoun *she* to avoid offending them," I confirm, just in case I'm wrong.

"No!"

"But you just —"

"Yes, that one over there is a *she* because she is a *woman*. Not all humans are women, Anax. You refer to men with *he*, or *him* or *his*."

"What's the difference?"

Frederick sighs, then begins to outline differences. All of them involve appearances, some of which I cannot even make out. I do not understand.

"Which are you?" I ask eventually. Even if I can't work out how not to offend most humans, I can at least learn not to offend my friend.

"He."

We approach the lone human – the lone woman – and Frederick introduces us in stammering Dutch that I have taught him. Like all humans in this reality, it is not convinced at first, but by the end of the conversation, it – she – leaves having made two more friends.

At the shore, Frederick hires a boat. It – he – doesn't have to row; I hold on to the boat with what's left of my strength, and it cuts across the water in my wake. Frederick gets out its violin and plays for me during my last miles, and it makes my aches and pains more bearable.

Once we are back on English shore I am forced to let go of the boat. Frederick reaches for my hand so that I may continue to bring it with me, but it is not fast enough. It calls after me as I leave it behind. I lose sight of it before I am even fifty metres away.

So it is that when I reach that London art gallery once again, I am alone, and there is no music to sooth my sore limbs or distract from my breathlessness. Death takes me, and all I can feel is relief.

So this is to be a life of snow, sea and sunsets.

There are fewer humans this far north, though to my relief, I am not so far north that there are none. Russia stretches out around me and I dash through time, trying to warn humans about bad winters and approaching storms.

None of them hear me. It's worse than before.

I pass through Finland, Sweden and Norway without a single human acknowledging me no matter how much I try to help, no matter how much I talk, no matter how loud I shout.

In this reality, no-one believes in me. I might as well not exist.

I do not blame them for their disbelief. How can I, when they are what I live for? What else am I to do with my thousands of lives other than watch the lives of the humans unfold?

In 1827 in a tavern in Reykjavik, I find a human I recognise instantly. A spark of hope awakens inside me. Humans do not remember previous realities as we time spirits do – they may not even exist in them. However, I would assume their personalities remain mostly the same. But if a human believed in me in my last life, then perhaps it will believe in me in this one too.

He, I remind myself. Frederick is a he.

"What are you drinking?" I ask in English, unsure if he will understand Icelandic.

The human jumps and turns, looking for a face to account for the voice. Relief floods me: it heard me!

It – he – hesitates. Then: "Anax?"

I freeze, speechless. I haven't seen him before in this reality. This is impossible.

"Frederick, how —?"

"I dreamed about you," he interrupts. "I suppose this means my dreams were true, as I suspected. Unless, of course, I'm hallucinating."

At least I won't have to explain everything to him again.

"I was given to understand that hallucinations are visible, and I am not."

His face contorts in the way that seems to indicate a human is happy. "Touché." He takes a drink. "So what's different to the last reality in which we met?"

"You're the first human to even notice me. They don't hear me even when I scream in their ears – not a single one."

"And, if I remember rightly, you and all your kind will be removed to the Land Of The Forgotten should humans lose belief in you?"

"I believe so."

"Then we have a problem on our hands." He drains his tankard and pays the bartender. "So what are we waiting for?"

Frederick and I agree it would be easier to meet at various points along my line of latitude rather than to travel together. We meet at dusk, for of course it must be dusk or I will be unable to meet them at all. This time around, sunset is my entire life.

He brings various guests with him to each meeting. Since Frederick has already explained everything before I talk to them, every single human he brings to me believes me. While it may be true that Frederick's friends are the only humans who even hear me, it is enough to give me hope.

❖

In all directions, all I can make out is white on the ground and blue in the sky. The air smells of nothing more than ice, and it tries to rip out my lungs as I breathe it out. It always reminds me of the fact that humans call this time the ice age; the name makes sense.

To time spirits, though, it's the meeting time.

I have heard about species-wide meetings being called in the realities before I existed, but this is the first one I have ever attended. The time spirit closest to me on the northern side, whose name is Stafra and who smells of coconut, tells me it isn't serious, and the elders simply wish to hear any significant reports anyone might have to give. Considering that one of these meetings has never been called during my existence, I highly doubt that.

It is a chaotic affair, to say the least. Every time spirit participates in passing messages up and down our line of longitude. It takes miles just for one report to reach the elders, assuming that it isn't repeated incorrectly and passed back for correction, or held up by the addition of several more reports along the way. But despite its inefficiencies, this is the only way to ensure that the elders hear every significant report, and every time spirit gets the elders' message.

After miles upon miles of passing along observations about the changing climate in recent realities, stories about being repeatedly and constantly ignored by humans (I am glad to find I am not the only one who noticed), and complaints about how cold the meeting time is, we finally receive the message from the elders. Stafra has launched into a tale of their search for the new time spirits who formed from the remains of their late sibling when the time spirit south of me interrupts earlier than expected.

The message is a short one. "Engage the humans!" the time spirit shouts to me. I turn back to the north and repeat the words to Stafra.

"I knew this situation with the humans was bad," Stafra comments after they have passed the message along. "But it's clearly worse than I thought it was."

I agree, then make my excuses to leave. I need to find Frederick.

I next see Frederick in Queensland, Australia, three lives later and amazed we have all made it so long with so little belief. Orders to engage the humans do no good when the humans can't hear you. Every time I am reborn, I fully expect to see a veil of darkness, or some fiery hell, or an unnavigable mist. I don't know what I expect the Land of the Forgotten to be like, but I definitely do not expect to find myself back in the human world.

It is midday and the middle of summer, and yet cold overtakes me as soon as I see him. I've had so much hope of seeing him over the last three lives, but if I had thought it impossible for him to remember me the first time, surely it is twice as unlikely for him to remember me a second time.

And there's always the chance he isn't the same Frederick he was in the previous realities.

But I know I cannot give up this opportunity just to spare my emotions.

"Frederick?"

He makes no sign that he has heard me. My breath goes short. I try again, trying to keep my voice from sounding too frantic. He pauses and cocks his head, listening. When I say his name a third time, he looks around. When he recognises my voice, his face drains of colour.

It takes him a little while to get his head around the fact that he's conversing with someone he met in a dream. Once he's calmed down, I ask if he'll help me like he did last time. He says,

"Help you with what?"

My breath hitches. If Frederick doesn't help me save my kind, I'm almost certain no-one else will.

"In the last reality we met in," I remind him, "You helped me convince other humans of my existence. So that my kind wouldn't end up in the Land of the

Forgotten. Frederick, it worked – we're still here! But this is not that reality, and we're still being forgotten. Please, will you help me?"

Frederick flounders for a moment before he replies. "I apologise, but this isn't my problem. I cannot disrupt my life to go running around the world helping ghosts who I met in dreams. And, if you will, I'd rather you addressed me as Mister Morris."

I gape. "But I… Please, Frederi – Mister Morris, you won't –"

"It is not my problem," he repeats. "Find someone else to do it."

I feel like I have been walked through.

I remind myself that I was stupid if I thought he would be able to keep his promise to always believe in me. More than stupid. I knew that if the rest of the world changes from reality to reality, then so must humans. I knew that time spirits are the only creatures who remember previous realities. And yet, somehow, stupidly, I hoped none of that would affect Frederick.

I sigh. I cannot berate myself for hoping. After all, it's all I have left now.

When my time for death comes again, I welcome the darkness with hope. I hope that I will see Frederick again. I hope that he will be back to the Frederick I know, the Frederick who has faith in me and keeps me company and plays the most beautiful violin. I hope he will help me prevent whatever fate may await us in the Land of the Forgotten. It's the not knowing that scares me most. What could possibly happen to creatures that don't exist?

This is a life of being walked through. The sensation doesn't even sicken me as much as it used to. I'm not worried, though – at least, no more worried than I already was. I've had several lives like this now, and we're still here.

There has been no sign of the sun since we were reborn; the time of night makes encountering humans to engage more difficult. It brings to mind the human saying "it's always darkest just before the dawn", and I repeat those words to myself as I flit through the 1820s, searching.

In Vienna in 1827, I find who I'm looking for.

"Frederick?"

He's on the other side of the street. Perhaps I'm just not loud enough or close enough.

"Frederick Morris! Frederick!"

Maybe it isn't him. Maybe it's someone else. It isn't exactly difficult, to mistake one human for another. But he stops to talk to someone and it's his voice. I stand right next to him and shout into his ear.

He cannot hear me.

The light has barely settled before me as I materialise in this new reality, when I hear a voice I recognise close by.

"Anax?"

"Ral?"

"Where are we? I don't recognise the time or place."

The view clears. The land is flat and dry from horizon to horizon, like a desert, except that the mist is far too cold for this to be a desert. Far above us, the sky is completely cloudless and yet also completely grey.

"I have no idea."

There are other voices. Other presences around us. I have never felt or heard so many time spirits in one time and place before. I feel crowded, surrounded, claustrophobic. And when I try to move, to skip through time to sometime more secluded – I cannot. I cannot move.

I cannot move.

"Anax." Ral's whisper is terrified. "There's no time here."

No time. No humans. Every direction looks the same – where are we? – and I already feel tired and achy and old – will I die already?

And then I know.

We will not die. This is the Land Of The Forgotten. This is a prison with no walls. This is where the forgotten things go.

~o~

I had a lot more time to write and a lot more ideas in my early teens, and though I haven't worked on the stories I wrote then for years, I don't like to think that I've abandoned them. I prefer to think that I'll come back to them one day, when I have both more life experience and more writing experience. So when I was trying to come up with something to write a short story on, I thought back to a story I wrote when I was about thirteen, called *The Land Of The Forgotten*. The creatures I wrote about in that story were humanoid beings with psychic abilities and super senses, which was quite generic. The only thing about them that I kept the same was their ability to reincarnate; everything else, I changed. In making the time spirits genderless, I hoped to provoke thought about gender and its arbitrariness. It also made writing from the point of view of a time spirit a bit of a challenge, especially when remembering to use non-gendered pronouns.

# HANNAH MICKLEBURGH
## NOW I WILL BELIEVE THAT THERE ARE UNICORNS

Hannah is an eighteen-year-old student from the Calder Valley in West Yorkshire, currently reading English Literature and Film Studies at the University of Surrey. Having been encouraged to get published from the tender age of eight and following up with attempts at poetry a few years later, short stories was the next stepping stone to something longer. She hopes to make a living by somehow combining journalism, screenwriting, and acting.

I am dead.

Go. I'll. Those are the two shortest complete sentences in the English language. I taught myself English and then I chose to spend time working those out. People – and by people I mean no person I know, but I'm sure there are many, and I envisage them debating this way in my head with their upturned noses and their saggy lips and their receding hairlines smelling of tea tree oil – say that scientific subjects are preferable over humanities for the reason that the answers are definite, factual, and less subjective or open to interpretation, that by memory alone they can gain full marks. While this is true, the former I disagree with, for the following reason: language, i.e. used in every essay-writing, creative, subject, is the most strictly defined thing that I know. Scientists, and I know this, admit that nothing is truly factual in their areas, but the most accurate theory they have.

They also say that it's unlikely they'll ever know the 'right' answer to the 'big' questions. Those are adjectives, but they are ambiguous. I don't like ambiguous.

I am ambiguous.

Unclear, undefined. Those are synonyms – noun. 'Noun' is a noun, but so is 'verb'. I don't like… I am ambiguous. That's scary. I don't like ambiguous. Doctors are scientists and scientists admit that it's unlikely they'll ever know exactly what's broken in minds, what creates or causes or *is* mental illness. So I'm ambiguous, because we're not dealing with the physical. A broken bone is a broken bone, but I don't have a broken bone.

I am broken.

Go. I'll. I know about extended sentences, where two or more sentences can be joined with conjunctions to make one, continuous, sentence. I prefer, and this is simply personal opinion, to think of my short sentences as dialogue.

"Go."

I am gone.

**Alex is crazy, and that's the first thing you should know, because it is important. I tell Alex to go and Alex listens to me, and if you knew me you'd know that that's the craziest thing ever because nobody should listen to me. I am here, I am whole, I am clear. I am *alive*.**

I am going to start high school. I am going to start high school late. I am going to start high school later than everybody else, and I am going to start high school later than everybody else in my year. I am going to start high school in the November of the year I should be halfway finished with *high school*. I am going to start high school in five, four, three, two, 1…

I am stupid.

**Alex is stupid, I am clever. Alex should hit the boy who got asked – when only Alex's hand was raised – instead and had the right answer when Alex didn't. Alex should hit Alex, too, for not having the right answer.**

I don't like ambiguous. Hitting is not ambiguous, but THAT QUESTION *WAS* AMBIGUOUS.

"Ouch," I exclaim, because the teacher taught our class about alternative words to use in a reporting clause, even if I don't trust teachers, "my hand hurts." I say this because my right hand is bandaged, because my right hand is stronger than my left hand, and I am not a freak (and now for clarity, because my writing is often mangled first time, I was called a freak and thus hit someone). Everybody in the world gets a little urge to just screw their hand up into a fist or wave it in the air like they just don't care. I don't have to comply with these urges, but I'm asked to – I am told to, and I choose to. I CHOOSE TO.

I am free.

I am not 'schizo', I am not 'bipolar' (nor 'bi', because I've heard that one before and I am told that it is not a shortened version of 'bipolar' – as 'schizo' is of schizophrenic, but 'schizo' is used in place of mad. As is 'freak'). I am not a freak. I have Borderline Personality Disorder, but I'm told to just calmly say; "No, I'm just BPD" whenever somebody claims I'm something I'm not, because it's more imposing, people don't know what to make of it, it's creepy and when I smile creepily afterwards and stare down the somebody until the somebody runs away it's because I want to. "Somebody" I think, because I can actually think myself, "some *bodies*" and the thought pleases me. It is appealing to me, but I do nothing, because I DO WHAT I WANT TO DO. The second non-finite verb, 'do', is redundant, and I am not angry. I'm just BPD.

**Alex is *just* BPD, and Alex knows what that means and still Alex can't control it. I am trapped. I am not a figment of the imagination; the imagination is a figment of me.**

**I am Alex.**

I am Alex.

I have a friend. I was given a friend, and now I have a friend because I was given a friend. This friend was given me. This friend is not really a friend, because I am not well acquainted with and do not trust them. These are important; not everything is, but these things are if you want to be a friend. My friend is a boy. My friend is my age. My friend is in my class; which doesn't make sense, really. Apparently they're stupid, which I can empathise with. I researched what empathy is because people – people I know and people I don't, all people (or at least normal people) – have empathy for their friends. As friends go, I can tick One out of Three boxes, which isn't bad, really. That's a third, one third, because I was taught about fractions today and it is a third because it *just is*, which isn't ambiguous at all. My friend was sarcastic today, so I learnt what sarcasm is, also. A third of people have cancer. That's a lot. That's sad. That's sympathy, which is different to empathy. They both include '-pathy' – both words, I mean. Some people – people I do not know, but which I would recognise in a criminal line-up – have called me that. I know that it either is short for 'psychopath' or 'pathologically really messed up'.

I am neither.

**I am both, which is sad. I want to tap the rhythm of 'Asleep' by The Smiths now.** *I want to go to bed.*

I want to get up. I cannot get up, because I don't *really* want to get up. THIS IS HOW IT WORKS. Urges, but I do what I want to do. Things are more tempting now, but I don't go to school anymore, and so I am not tempted to hit stupid people (everyone in my year is stupid, I've figured, because me and my friend are in it and we are stupid). I don't need to get up.

**I need to get up, because when I am not up I am normal. I am nearly normal, I still have the memory of myself when I am not up; it is a dream. Dreams are good. I am good.**

I am bad.

Now I follow my urges, not lead. Temptations are… tempting. They are bad. But, if I am bad, surely I must go with things that are bad? I want to follow my urges, the temptations. We are good.

I am good.

## Now I Will Believe That There Are Unicorns

I am in control again. I have another friend, this one only tells me to be friends with my friend, though, so they're not much of a friend. They're not *my* friend, but they are right. My friend tells me to listen to the other friend, which I did in the first place (obviously). I just want to go for a jog. I am going for a jog, but my friend is intercepting me, they're telling me not to go. I am yelling at them.

I am angry.

"You haven't even a jacket." I pull a bin bag over my head in answer and set off. "Your laces are untied." I turn to my friend and jog backwards in smaller steps, sticking my tongue out. My friend cannot see my tongue, because I have a bin bag over my head. I pull it down and it rips and he can see my tongue. He chuckles, sets off after me. I speed up and he doesn't catch me up. I am darting down the road and I don't know where I am going but the day is beautiful: the clouds remind me of candy floss, even though candy floss is pink – but they are too soft and wispy to be compared to cotton wool. They float through the sky majestically, which is not what I do when I fall. I flail through the sky unceremoniously. My friend catches me up and helps me up, gently supporting me. He brushes off my knees, my joggers, and then ties the laces of my trainers. I am not angry. Not anymore.

I am happy.

We are dancing through the sky beautifully; the sky is exploding with colour and all of my favourite things. I didn't know that I had favourite things but as I waltz through the labyrinth of rainbows and heavy metal I understand that I *like* these things. I like rainbows because they make the best of the rain, and because colours are bright and grey is ambiguous. I like heavy metal because good music makes me sad, and I don't like being sad. I do like good music, too, though, and 'Lucy in the Sky with Diamonds' by The Beatles begins playing over everything, which is wholly inappropriate because we are Alex and friend, not Lucy and diamonds. A dog with a diamond encrusted collar jumps down at me from out of another cloud – this one is pink – and suddenly we are no longer dancing. I don't know where my friend has gone; but I want to, and so he pops up behind me and we play with the dog and for some reason I want to call it Fru-Fru so, when my friend reaches out and scares her away (he's never been good with animals), I call the name and she comes. I smile at my friend.

I am happy.

I had clinical depression, which was caused by my BPD, which is ridiculous and wrong, as far as I'm concerned, because one disorder should not cause another because then they are ganging up on you and that's not right. Or so says the other friend, who I neither empathise nor am acquainted well with, but who I do trust. She, because it's a lady with wavy magenta hair (like Ramona Flowers, but I don't think she'd understand the reference), says that I no longer have depression. I didn't feel particularly elated when I got the news, and so I don't know whether it's true or if I'm not trying to trick them; she laughed at this, and I didn't understand why.

I am new.

My friend is now giving me a hug. I don't remember him getting a snazzy motorbike but he has one and I like it, and he brought me here on it. Now that he's hugging me, he sifts his fingers through my hair like it's liquid gold, so I'm a cat, purring and scratching into the touch; he weaves his fingers like they're yarn through the golden thread of my hair and when I metamorphose into Fru-Fru and try to back away he's lifting bundles of it, King Midas turning the threads to solid blocks of gold. He spins me around and it's like we're back in the clouds and I'm looking down at the shadow of my mind. He points out the towering landmarks of what I once was and I call on all my new-found powers of Zeus to topple them but I don't because that's self-destructive and we need reminders of our past because it's a constant. My friend brings me back down to Earth and asks if I would like hot chocolate before school, because he managed to scavenge a job at a coffee shop at some point and I've started high school again – first year, afternoons. I'm better in the afternoons. We speed off towards the nice-smelling part of town (this part smells innately *wrong*. I associate it with wrong) and I wrap my friend in a rib-crushing hug. I hear the bittersweet chords of 'Imagine' by John Lennon strum melancholically through the empty orchestra of my mind and must fill it with the sorrowful song myself. I smile a grimace.

I am alive.

~o~

The piece was originally composed, in mostly full form, as part of my year 12 English Language AS coursework from an idea I had for a story or film even before then. Some style models I used, and which influenced even that first spark of an idea, were things like the film adaptations of Chbosky's *The Perks of Being a Wallflower* and Quick's *Silver Linings Playbook*. You could say that despite this, the style that really motivates me is beat writing. It may therefore be unsurprising that some parts of my work are edited for general comprehensibility. There are also some parts in this version of the short story that were cut from my coursework, and it has been edited for a British audience, but it only improves the overall storytelling; what interests me most in this piece is the frank discussion of mental health and, of course, the way in which this is presented. There are very few works that dare touch on such topics, and even fewer that go beyond depression and bipolar disorder, and so being able to introduce an almost entirely unique frame for my character's development is of great interest to me - as is the style, conveying this disorder through the character's own voices. In ways the text can seem audience-less, not narrated in any person nor as if to be read, but in other ways it is intrinsically metafictional, the voice conversing with the reader about what has been written before. Writing for me has always been about showing a story I want to be preserved, and time both in and out of classes have helped me hone a way to not only show the physical world of the story but to use symbols, allusions and references, style and all manner of other things (my favourite being a dreaded dash of figurative language) in order to reveal more. What has been left out is equally important; one must always read between the lines, but also off the page and down the backwater in the gaps left even there.

# STEPHANIE GALLON
## DOTTY GRIM AND THE RED-HOODED HERRING

Stephanie Gallon is a twenty-two-year-old writer from Blyth, Northumberland. Graduating with First Class Honours in English and Creative Writing from the University of Sunderland, she has previously had her poetry and short stories published. She is also a blogger with PhD aspirations and a great love of Twitter.

When people have a problem, they find their way to The Village End Book Shop. It doesn't matter which end of The Village they try to find the shop: north, east, south or west, it is always waiting for them. That's the magic of the shop; it knows how to find the lost. And if the lost are looking for answers or someone to help, then all they have to do walk to the back room and up the rickety stairs to the glass pane door. That's where they'll find me.

My name is Dorothea Grimm. No one calls me that though. For as long as I can remember, everyone has called me Dotty. I'm a Private Detective for the Ever After Detective Agency, the last resort for a lot of folk around here. When no one else takes them seriously, I always do. That sort of reputation attracts small cases: lost kittens and missing bracelets, little things like that. My biggest case, my first real case, came mid-autumn last year.

It was an ordinary day in Marchen. The sun was bright, filtering through the blinds of my office, and the room was uncomfortably warm for an October day. I was bored out of my mind. I had read that morning's paper at least ten times, rearranged my files alphabetically, then by colour, then by chronology, then… well, you get the idea. There's only so many ways you can arrange files and I had done them all.

I was in the middle of my twelfth unsuccessful game of solitaire, wondering if I was bored enough to clean fifty years of dust from the cabinets, when there was a knock on the door. I quickly pushed my cards in to the top drawer and hurried to answer it.

'Welcome to the Ever After Detective Agency. How can I help you?' I asked with my warmest smile.

Standing there was an old woman. I was sure I had seen her before, but I couldn't place the face. She had white hair and small, half-rim glasses perched at the end of her nose. She was pale and looked uneasy. Despite the heat, she was wrapped tightly in the most beautiful shawl I had ever seen; it was black, and it glittered like the night sky. In her wrinkled hands, she held a book.

'I don't know if you can help me,' she said finally, her voice barely rising above a whisper.

'We can always help if you need it.' I led her through to my office. It was a bit of a tight squeeze with filing cabinets all around us. It used to be a storage cupboard, but she didn't need to know she was sitting where the mop used to live. 'What's your name?'

The old woman's voice was trembling. 'I'm Granny. Granny Hood?'

Then I remembered the half-page ad I'd seen in *The Marchen Mirror*. The woman in the picture looked happier than the one in front of me. Granny's Craft Boutique was one of the oldest and most popular businesses in The Village, and they were celebrating their fifty-year anniversary with a huge sale event. It was meant to be the biggest party The Village had ever seen.

'I'm such a big fan. I love your boutique, I got my favourite coat there.' I smiled at her. 'I'm Dotty. What can I do for you?'

'My granddaughter, Harmony,' Granny burst in to tears. 'She didn't come over last night.'

A missing person. That was a first. I offered her a tissue from the box I kept on-hand. She took a fistful. 'And is that unusual?'

'Yes! She left her mother's house and was meant to come straight to me. She knows not to leave the path and come directly to me so she doesn't get lost.

She's a good girl and she always does what she's told.' Granny blew her nose and continued. 'We were going to take pictures for the catalogue. She was my favourite little model. Everyone always tells me how beautiful she looks.' She put the book down on the desk and flipped to the back.

There were dozens of pictures of a striking young girl. She had bright green eyes and soft-looking auburn curls, which framed her face. Her smile was bright and infectious; it was easy to see why she had been chosen to model.

'Is this the most recent picture you have?'

'Yes. It's a candid from our summer collection. I just loved how her hair looked in that one; all curly and cute. We called the police, but they said she's not missing yet. They won't do anything. They said she probably got lost or went to a friend's house. But she's just a little girl and I know something is not right. She would never wander off on her own; it's dangerous in the woods. Something awful must have happened.'

I didn't say anything to that. Everyone in Marchen knew never to venture off the path after dark; it was common knowledge that monsters lurked in the shadows.

'Can I have one of these photos?' I took one with permission and put it on an empty file. 'Don't worry, Granny. Dotty Grimm is on the case. We'll find her.'

Granny beamed. I could see the family resemblance when she smiled; she looked twenty years younger. 'Thank you, thank you so much. We'll pay anything if you find her. Thank you.'

'I just need to ask you some questions if that's alright.' I grabbed my trusty pen and notepad. 'What's your granddaughter's full name?'

'Harmony Jane Hood. But we've always just called her Red.'

~o~

*Dotty Grimm and the Red-Hooded Herring* is a passion project of mine that I have been wanting to write for almost a year now. It embodies my two favourite genres: fairy tales and crime fiction. They intersect in some of my favourite features: archetypal characters, warnings for the reader, and the inevitable clash of good vs evil. *Dotty Grimm and the Red-Hooded Herring* talks about a crime in a world where the magical is mundane. She lives in a shop which moves around the village. It is a world where crime still exists because evil and malice does. I am a big fan of Dotty, her friends and the adventures they share. I *hope* to one day see the finished novel in print.

# HARRY DRAPER
## LAST TIME

Harry Draper is a nineteen-year-old writer, originally from Bristol. Currently studying Creative Writing at Edge Hill University, he has previously been published in the *Usborne Young Writer's Magazine* and the *Young Writer's Mini Saga* book and is currently working at the Edge Hill University Literary Press on its first publication. His hobbies include writing Doctor Who scripts and stop motion animation.

13th November. The Man woke up one day. The one day. The same day as the day before. And the Man found himself waking up the same, as he had done so many times before.

Breakfast. He could have buttered his toast on the other side for a change. But he'd had that very same idea of change so many times before, it would hardly have felt like a change at all. So the same side as before.

The news was never really news to him. Divorce settlements and the economy and a murder and the Mona Lisa and water on Mars and LEGO and pandas giving birth. That was the beauty of the licence fee; you always paid, because you always knew what you were going to receive.

They should give the news a new name, the Man thought. The Olds. Or the Sames. 'Hello and welcome to the Sames. Our top story today, yesterday and tomorrow…' Now that would really be news, thought the Man.

But then the Man remembered that he had had this exact same thought yesterday. They should give thoughts a new name, the Man thought. And no doubt that had been what he had thought last time. But that was the beauty of the brain; you always let it think, because you always knew what you were going to think.

New messages on the voicemail. All the same voices, saying the same things as before.

Outside. Cold in February. And next door's Springer Spaniels. Always the same conversations, at the break of dawn. 'Woof, woof. Woof, woof, woof, woof. Woof.' The Man could hardly hear himself think. What was that you thought? the Man thought. I CAN HARDLY HEAR MYSELF THINK, he thought again.

Driving the car. The same lights were shining – well, not really shining, more…existing – to pace him along his way. Red, yellow, green. The Man tuned in to Radio SameAsBe4. A new No. 1, eh? I'll be the judge of that, he thought. Judge, jury and executioner.

The Bank. Another day at work. The one day at work. Queues. Stamp the cheque. Bit of printing. All of that was fine. Everybody took an interest. Money made the world go round, over and over again, each and every day. That was the beauty of money; everybody needs it, so everybody came.

But what was odd was that the Man would look at the faces on the other side of the glass - and smile. Because he knew, for a cosmic reason that he would never understand, he would never see those faces again. Every day, the faces were always new. Nobody was the same as last time.

But that was still not enough. Life was still the same.

Perhaps I could punch one of them in the face? the Man would often think, as he smiled politely to the people paying in their cheques. He never did punch any of them in the face. But he kept imagining it, not as a 'fist-in-the-face' affair with shards of glass and a pool of blood and screaming and police sirens. Just a punch to shake things up. However, if fantasy ever did bleed into reality, not only would that be unlike anything that had happened last time, it really would be his last time at the Bank. The end of his life as he knew it.

It's a miracle he never did punch anyone in the face.

It had happened again. The Man had buried himself into his thoughts so much, like pictures within pictures within pictures. The Droste effect had taken effect, surprise surprise. Just like last time. In reality, in the here and now, the Man had to confront the Manager.

'Pull yourself together, Man!" the Manager would say. The Manager managed the Man with fury, passion and two hands that shook him like a ragdoll. It was ironic whenever the Manager said that, the Man always thought. With those two hands, the Manager seemed to pull the Man together pretty well enough. Or rather, the Manager would tear the Man apart and then pull him back together afterwards. But the Man was grateful for the Manager. The Manager could never manage himself.

The spilt cup of coffee. Using up all the ink cartridges in the photocopier on one document. The malfunctioning fire alarm. The second spilt cup of coffee. He was such an idiot. Eventually, the emergencies weren't even interesting any more. They were all the same as each other. And it was enough to make him cry, each and every time.

18th October. One day, something happened. Something that really was news. A headline even. One day, the Man thought something very interesting indeed. The one day he felt something brand new. The one day he said something very important.

'I love you,' said the Man.

'Oh,' said the Manager. And then she smiled. And, in that moment, the Man knew that he had been forgiven for spilling all those cups of coffee over her trousers.

15th April. The Man woke up one day. The one day.

Breakfast, and he was hungry like the wolf. Toast. Which side to butter? Why not both? It's not like life could get any madder.

And suddenly, the news was news to him, in this brand new world of his. The bees coming back. Blackpool in the World Cup. Exotic new species of bird, screeching their mating calls, unlike anything he'd seen the last time he'd cast his eyes to the iPlayer.

Loads more voicemail messages than usual. But they were probably all the same as each other and the same messages as last time. Ah well. Delete.

Outside. Warm in April. 'Woof, woof, woof, woof. Woof, woof'. Ha. Cheers, thought the Man, as he smiled.

He drove. And suddenly, those lights by the side of the road, pacing him – they were not simply existing, more…shining. They were perfectly cut jewels. Ruby, gold, emerald.

All these corridors looked the same, and the Man still felt lost. Wandering aimlessly. The one bird who flusters and panics. But he heard her. The Manager was taking care of the business. Life's transaction. Her deposit. Very painful. She cried. And he waited.

The Man looks through the glass. And although she is one of many, some smiling, some crying, on the other side of the glass, the Man keeps looking. All his life he's wanted to take out the loan, even though he knows it will be painful. That's the thing about loans; they always end. One day.

But this is the here and now, and here she is, new born and blinking. The Man felt born again himself. Because when you're born, it's like the whole word is born in that very moment. You never feel – you never can feel – that it's existed before you ever did. All that history and backstory and past, it's all stamped into the books, ready-made. The world itself is pulped and printed and published, first edition.

But the Man hadn't managed things very well. He had risked losing her. He had risked terminating the loan before it even began.

She is his - but it doesn't feel like it. The possibility of no loan at all. Very painful. He cries. And she waits.

No story is ever the same. But all of them end the same. One last full stop.

No, thinks the Man.

What do you mean, no?

I mean no, the Man thinks again. It's the same thought over and over again. The same as last time.

He could have been any man. The Weatherman. The Spaceman. The Roman. The Sandman. The Crooked Man. The Hitman. The Batman. A Madman. A Bad Man. A Sad Man. Once he could have depended upon the news never being news to him and the voicemail recording his life for training purposes and his brain ticking over the same thoughts. At the very least, he could have lived the life and died the death of the Glad Man. But now, he knew the Man he was going to be.

This time, unlike any last time before, and for the rest of his life, he was going to be the Dad Man.

~o~

*Last Time* began as an exercise written in a class at University about Miranda July. We were pouring over the pages of *No One Belongs Here More than You*, and, admittedly, it took me a while to immerse myself in them. However, I began to find July's prose striking and eye-catching. Her writing is both acutely structured with precision and liberated at the same time and her characters are fascinatingly presented as being isolated and entrapped within their emotions. The lack of identity attributed to many of these characters struck me as interesting and was the catalyst for the creation of the *Man and the Manager*. As I began writing my exercise based upon July's style, the joke about the News desperately needing a new name – 'the Sames' – formed and, rather taken with it, I carried on writing. *Last Time* was the result. Whilst I do not commonly write in this more 'abstract' form, I love characters coming to life in front of me, whether they're on a street or a spaceship. And whilst this might be my only dip into this particular pool of writing, it's been the most refreshing dip. This story definitely owes its origins to Miranda July's strange and sterling world. Many thanks must also go to the staff at Edge Hill for their great support and my fellow students, who are already shaping up to be the most wonderful writers the future could ask for. Ultimately, the biggest thanks must go to my Mum. (I know this is cliché but it is a lovely cliché.) Her eagerness for the next page kept me tapping away at the laptop. When she was moved by the last line about the Dad Man, I smiled. I love writing. I love writing for her even more.

# LEXY HUDSON
## WELL VERSED

Lexy grew up in London, graduated with a First-class Bachelor's in English and Philosophy from the University of York in July 2015, and has since worked in a variety of literary and arts administration settings. Her collections of short stories, some of which have been published in print, can be found in connection with her Twitter account. *Well Versed* is her first full-length novel, and she is at work on a second. When not seeking agent representation, Lexy invests a great deal of time and money in books and caffeinated beverages.

It was Crusoe's turn to do the coffee run that morning. After eighteen months at the Technological Institute of the Metropolitan City of London - affectionately shortened to 'TIM' - she had mastered the art of balancing a tray of drinks in one hand, and using the other to swipe a laminated tag at the correct angle to get her from the reception, and the on-site Goldbean, to the labs.

The turnstile clicked and a green circle blinked. She disappeared around a muted silver pillar, retreating into a narrative entirely closed off from the constant flow of people on noisy streets.

'Morning,' said a bear-like security guard - one of many - in a powder white shirt, presumably also one of many.

'Morning,' she said, her flexed hand aching under the weight of six cups. Crusoe stopped at a set of polished white enamel doors and punched in the code for the main floor, which was different from the nine other codes she had committed to memory, after some inevitable trial and error in her first week. Every other set of doors needed an access code or card scan or card swipe and every single staff member found it exhausting, however necessary.

One descent in a left later, bringing her firmly underground, Crusoe exchanged her spring jacket for a clear sheet of plastic with arms - a departure from traditional white lab garb. She was convinced this was TIM's attempt to brand itself as cutting-edge, ahead of the curve, quirky but respectable, hipster. *Hipster TIM*. She chuckled to herself while opening the final glass door inwards.

'Knew you'd be up,' she said.

Nandita, the most eager-to-please junior member of the team, had been on night duty. From past experience, Crusoe suspected she'd worked flat through the hours without even noticing, but it could happen to anyone: the lab was uniformly fluorescent, windowless, and overrun with screens. Human or machine, there was always something at work.

Crusoe wasn't a particularly loud speaker, but the spacious acoustics sent her voice bouncing off the furthest wall and onto the back of Nandita's bent neck.

'Oh, hi. Erm, morning. Is it morning?'

''Tis indeed.'

'Oh, wow.' Nandita uncurled from her workstation, grey-ringed eyes screwed shut as a yawn escaped her mouth. Dazedly, she smoothed down ridges of bunched plastic in the creases of her elbows.

'Something tells me the nuclear apocalypse could unfurl around the building and you still wouldn't be distracted from your stats.'

'I know, not healthy is it,' mumbled Nandita, sliding up and off her chair. She slipped her hands into clear pockets, which to Crusoe was a notable design flaw - the very act of putting hands in pockets became strangely futile, like a child putting their hands over their face instead of hiding.

Crusoe studied the markings on the side of one tall white cup, inferred it was her skinny doubleshot cappuccino, and set it aside. She offered up Nandita's usual order: a tiny shot of espresso.

'Erm, no, no thanks I'd better not,' said Nandita, looking torn, 'I want to take a nap in the Nook, then I'll re-heat it or something. But, erm, thank you.'

'Sure, naps are key.'

Peeling off her lab coat, Nandita shuffled towards the Nook - a small, minimally furnished room for members of the team to rest in during and after long lab hours. There was one bed, a toilet, sink and shower, not unlike a prison cell. The plushy duck door stop counteracted that vibe.

While Nandita napped, Crusoe settled into a wheely chair, white to match the walls, and sipped her cappuccino as the rest of the team moved in and out of the lab like extras out of a movie frame:

'Cheers Crusoe.'

'Hey Loran.' A resident computer scientist: a large black Americano. This month her hair was the colour of sour cherries.

'Morning love.'

'Hiya Bob.' A black tea. Their lead astrophysicist hailed from Lancashire and stubbornly refused to invest in a hard coffee habit like the Londoners and South-Easterners.

'Crusooooe.'

'Daviiii.'

Her closest work friend, and owner of the full-fat extra shot latte, Davi was the only person with whom Crusoe had developed a secret handshake - it changed every other day according to an arbitrary pattern. He was also the only man she knew who could wear a bow tie and sweater vest without looking twee and, for a smoker, had an inexplicably pearly smile.

'How's it going?' he asked, voice like a whirring engine.

'Well, now that the weekend's behind us, I can say I've gone a full fortnight without getting a migraine, woohoo!'

Crusoe and Davi made jazz hands at the same time to commemorate the occasion.

'Excellent. You doing anything differently then?'

'No,' sighed Crusoe, 'alas, the identity of my trigger is in a universe millions of metaphysical planes from here.'

'At least you know it's not coffee.'

'If my migraines were triggered by coffee,' said Crusoe, dropping her voice to a mutter, 'I'd be fucked.'

Bob was working just behind her. He was relaxed about most things for a sixty-year-old, but swearing in the workplace was his grouchy old man pet peeve of choice.

'Right, onto some actual tasks.'

'Oh yeah, I forgot we have jobs,' said Davi. He and Crusoe tapped their coffee cups. 'Cheers.'

**Username:** PC19

**Password:** Nathan1104

As a teenager, Crusoe had spent the first fortnight of Nathan's existence not knowing where to stand in order to observe from a distance, or if she was allowed to observe at all. Nathan was a gift her mother and stepfather had made for themselves - for months she'd felt like a value erased from a chalkboard equation. It had been a strange time for her, living out her days at school in the familiar, status quo role of only child, before coming home every time and remembering that this way of thinking was obsolete: there was a fourth being in her family's world, and there always would be.

That is, until otherwise disproved.

Every time Crusoe used that login, she wondered if it was a mistake to use a password that would remind her of a little brother lost too soon. But the original, hard-hitting effect barely touched her now; the sadness was a little anchor on her heart that tugged, but then bobbed away with other places to be.

For the following six hours, the core team worked in concentric circles around the lab, separating and re-uniting like fluid pixels on a screensaver. However, their movements were limited: the Parallelodigm took up three-quarters of the entire room. Crusoe divided her time between her computer, other people's computers, and the machine's viewing windows.

Nandita emerged from the Nook in a far brighter state after her power nap. The youngest staff member (aside from the interns, several floors up), she was the only astrobiologist for this project at TIM. She had been the only student on her combined course at undergraduate level, and remained so for the following three years of postgraduate work.

Dr Crusoe was the resident astrophysical statistical engineer. The print on her ID card was very small.

Half of her day was spent lying horizontal on a wheeling board beneath the low silver curve of the Parallelodigm, sleek and stainless as the skin of a jet. With one knee up, the other straight out, and goggles on her face, Crusoe peered through an oval window no bigger than her forehead. Electric blue bands pulsated behind the glass, and from these regular, geometric, abstract lines, she drew meaning. Multiple meanings. Whole universes, in fact.

Crusoe did not get her Master's, her Doctorate, or a place on this project, for simply regurgitating everything that Hugh Everett and the other giants of quantum physics had already said. She got on for doing something original with the material, for nudging the dialogue forward and sending it snowballing.

The Parallelodigm began as the name of a thought experiment in response to other hypothetical particle generators and accelerators. From her thesis, to the grant applications, to the blueprints, to actuality, the name had stuck around. Much like TIM.

'How's it looking, Davi?'

'Conditions are more brittle in this one,' he replied from the largest screen in the room. It took up half of the back wall, dwarfing the binders, cables, manuals and assorted knick-knacks shelved below. Lines in a crescendo of neon hues curved and intersected according to their own choreography against a three-dimensional axis. At 116% zoom, they formed a geography textbook picture: a basic seafront, rising hills that became mountains, dotted with trees and capped with heavy snow. Pinprick maple birds flickered over the scene in a Sisyphean loop.

From a worktop at the back of the lab, surrounded by wires, Loran watched her computer periodically screenshot the wall-sized image. She put the tip of her thumb and index finger to her monitor and zoomed in on the white mountains.

'We calling this one 'Heavy Arctic', then?'

Davi wavered a deliberating hand in the air.

'Nah, not 'Heavy' - we've had heavier in earlier models. Maybe 'Moderate' instead.'

'Wonder how many visits to the Thesaurus tab we'll have racked up by the time this project's done,' Loran drawled, entering the title and moving on to the next screenshot. Now the picture showed a mostly volcanic landscape.

Differences between models weren't always so clear. If the landscape of one looked identical to another, Loran would select a different column of ppq (particles per miliquadrant) values to focus on from Davi's extensive selection on the shared drive. Zooming all the way down to 'Population', 'Residences', 'Flora' and 'Minerals' could reveal vast differences: the faceless avatars of humans and humanoids might be no taller than three feet in one, and have tails in another. Sometimes all it took to distinguish 'Green Model 1179' from 'Green Model 1180' was the presence, or absence, of a single flower.

Crusoe slid out from under the Parallelodigm and cricked her shoulders. She sidled up to a long black cylinder that helped to channel the inevitably mammoth amounts of energy for the bands from a generator, so boxy and dense it was almost a brute fact of nature, something which had sat there long before TIM's construction.

'I think we need the beam on a higher concentration,' she said to everyone who was listening, arms wrapped around the cylinder as though she were about to carry it on her shoulder.

'It's already on 4.6 billion volts,' said Bob, twirling his screen stylus like a biro.

'The bands are thinning,' said Crusoe, adjusting one dial, then another, with the precision of setting a watch. As an engineer, she was one of a handful authorized to do this herself. Though she couldn't see for herself how the lasers were shifting beneath the opaque black shell, Crusoe felt her palms warm and heard whirring from within. Any longing for babies were, if not dormant, then nonexistent, but she appreciated the sensation of something approximating a life beneath her fingertips.

The day speedily twisted to an end at five o'clock, leaving a bin of takeaway cups and scraps of number-adorned paper in its wake. The team wound down without ever shutting down, as was routine. Bob was set to monitor all incoming data overnight from the Nook. Crusoe would be on the night after that.

'Where do all these people go when they're not swarming the pavements?' Loran grumbled as she and Crusoe navigated the tide of commuters outside. They dodged as much contact with strangers as possible whilst heading for the same station.

'In Tokyo they have those business trip capsules that look like stacked washing machines from the outside,' said Crusoe. Hands in pockets, they trotted down deep stairs. 'Wonder if in a few years we'll have some of those.'

'Would bring my rent down like nobody's business,' said Loran, 'provided I could cram at least three screens in there.'

They parted ways at the North-South divide. Crusoe read the second half of a slightly out-of-date *In Science* to make the forty-minute return trip slide by unseen. Her mum posted an issue to her every weekend and, the following Friday, they mused about its content on the phone over their respective cups of tea.

Crusoe had no particular desire to inform her that she already had a subscription as one of her job perks - it made for meaty conversation between chitchat bookends, and she appreciated her mum making an effort to be a part of her shiny, new-fangled, history-in-the-making world.

Sometimes it went to Crusoe's head, on the occasion she was invited to speak for a podcast, or a news show breakfast segment, or as a documentary voxpop - it was always terribly exciting and glamourous for several days, and then as soon as the sessions were over, Crusoe would forget they had ever happened until a family friend emailed to say, 'we saw you on the telly!' two weeks later.

By the time underground became overground, London was dipped in a muted blue. Crusoe protected her ears from the evening chill by curtaining them with her hair.

'I'm home!' she announced to the empty flat, save for Acorn, her hedgehog. It achieved the desired effect: the pet stood to attention at his barred door and looked right up at Crusoe's face. She opened the little hatch, scooped him out, and set him on a cushion on her squishy indigo sofa.

Though vaguely oriented towards cats and dogs alike ("ambipetrous" was apparently the word for it), there had always been room in Crusoe's heart for a little ball of quills. She hadn't ever expected to own one, but when her former flatmate moved overseas to be with her Brazilian boyfriend, Crusoe had become the sole heir of her pet. Acorn was originally called Stewie, but Crusoe secretly despised the name, and had rechristened him as quickly as possible.

'We had an exciting day today, Acorn. Generated a model world whose coniferous plants all grew red leaves, and then one in which leaves didn't exist anywhere. Then, we had to zoom *way* in on two models that appeared to have identical topographies, infrastructures, cultures, everything. Nandita got everyone into a panic because she thought there was a glitch in the system. No no - in a bakery storeroom, somewhere on one of the continents, a cake box sat on a worktable. That was in one. In the other, it was upside-down on the floor. Remarkable, isn't it?' Crusoe watched Acorn scurry on the cushion in slow circles, wiggling his tiny nose. 'Guess you had to be there.'

She shrugged off her jacket, scarf and shoes, and went to the open kitchenette to make pasta with a mature cheddar sauce. She kept half an eye on Acorn at all times, but trusted him to enjoy leisure outside the cage responsibly. After her dinner she fed him his: dried mealworms, followed by shredded carrot for dessert.

That night, as on any other, Crusoe lay in the middle of her bed, sleepily pondering the dark. She followed strands of light bleeding up from the streets and imagined the ceiling was a black planetarium screen. There, the lights became universes, gliding, pinwheeling and almost colliding with one another. They were equal in their respective existences against indifferent and ominous dark matter.

Every night since starting at T.I.M., Crusoe had fallen asleep dizzy with anticipation at what she and the team would achieve, if not this decade, then the next. She dreamed of bringing universes together as long-lost relatives, identical save for microscopic, sub-atomic differences, descended from the same singularity at the beginning of all time and space.

She could think of no other, or better, way to fall asleep.

~o~

I've always been fascinated by parallel worlds discourse, but until last year, I had no clear way of working it into a story. Then I asked myself what an applied science of other worlds would look like, how we might conceive of physically travelling between them, and all the misadventures entailed therein. Following three protagonists and their quickly converging storylines, *Well Versed* is about the fine line between science and magic, about hypothetical worlds coming alive before our eyes, and about what it means to feel like an outsider while acting the part of someone who belongs. The opening chapter is standard high fantasy. The extract in this anthology is the second chapter, where the introduction of a parallel but entirely new narrative shows that this won't be quite the fantasy tale you expect.

I begin a new writing project when a "What if…?" question enters my head and sets up shop there. I enjoy writing in a combination of genres, where ideas can collide and rules for what a story may or may not do can be bent. I admire so many authors, but particular favourites are David Mitchell, Jennifer Egan, Haruki Murakami, Susanna Clarke and, of course, J.K. Rowling. Their work is rich and full of life, wit, style, substance and reading magic.

Writing is my compulsion and my raison d'être: there is no better medium for making sense of everything than the written word.

I write short fiction to experiment with ideas, genres and characters. The rest of the time, I work on novels. My dream is to find an agent and regularly publish fiction for, well, the rest of my days, all the while continuing to read as much as possible and refine my craft, because I'm sure there is a great deal more to learn.

# CJS WILLIAMS
## MEASURED IN COFFEE SPOONS

CJS Williams is a twenty-two-year-old student from southwest London. He has lived on almost every continent, but is now reading English and Creative Writing at Goldsmith's College, where he spends most of his time trying to avoid cliché. He has previously had his prose published in other magazines, and is currently working on starting his own publication. He loves the art of Francis Bacon and the films of David Lynch.

"I don't wanna do this anymore. I'm depressed."

"No you're not. How can you be?" I looked at him from around my laptop screen.

"I don't know. I just am."

While he was lying down on the couch, it struck me for the first time how similar we looked. He was facing away, burying his nose into the soft leather and breathing it in, his long mane drawn over his neck and shoulders. Except for the hair we really did have the same attributes; the glasses, the short beard that never seemed to go anywhere, the once athletic shape now turned to pudgy dogshit, and the adoption of bathrobes that sometimes turned to sweatpants when we felt formal.

"You can't be depressed." I paused, and realized that wasn't entirely fair. "Can people like you be depressed?"

He looked at me. "What do you mean people like me? How do you think that makes me feel?" He tried to get up but failed.

I don't remember where I first heard it. I could have made it up. I do that a lot at parties, I make up little anecdotes to prove my point. I talk about the post-Fabian novel and its effect on modern literature in order to expose the liars and the cheats; I discuss the importance of space travel to future generations, about the abandonment of conservative values by the Republican Party as they make a progressive lean to the left after the Reagan administration. Politics, literature, science, all of it. I am an absolute fraud. It's not as if I don't know that I am. Of course I know, it's just more fun this way. Even when I'm telling the truth I'm lying. I am, after all, a writer and that is what storytelling is: a lie, a fiction to bring out the more noble truths. There have been thousands of stories I have wanted to tell, and all of them touch upon some truth in one way or another. But for as long as I can remember, I have wanted to tell a story that will change our knowledge of everything. I have had a vision, maybe a waking dream or some sign from whatever all-powerful deity exists (I was, and still am, fashionably pantheist), of this image of the greatest story. It is the story of a priest, dressed in black, walking through a desert. A man (maybe he's a hunter or a trader) sees him, and behind the priest there is a mirage of the same priest. Now, ignoring all the laws of sight, imagine that the mirage of the priest is copied, over and over, cast infinitely into existence all the way across the desert, out of this world, out of our universe. And imagine being able to see it, from right where you sit. Would we all see the mirage? Would people from all over the world be able to see it, after it had been repeated enough? Infinity is no joke. Would the world be immediately overrun by priests in black? Sometimes, when I look up into the night sky, I think I see him out of the periphery of my vision, sometimes looking bored or reading a book, but mostly just walking. But whenever I turn my head, he's gone.

Here we find the issue. I have told the story to you already, and it only took around two hundred words. But it is weird stuff, an idea I picked up from somewhere when I was younger (probably in college when I was smoking pot with the rest of the useless children). And maybe I should explain about that part of my life.

## Measured In Coffee Spoons

I had been smoking weed for a month exactly, from February 1st to the 28th. I smoked every day, ranging from a single joint to bowls of the stuff, changing effects from being lightheaded and woozy to being passed out on the floor with marker on my face and beer cans stacked on top of me. I remember waking up on the first day of March, with new money in my bank account from my godfather, thinking, "everything is so clear". I stopped smoking. I joined the university magazine and I began to read voraciously, perhaps looking for evidence of the black priest, looking for him to walk into my room and begin a conversation with me. I read more; I realized there was an infinite source of wisdom in the pages of books, wisdom I could tap into if I could just spend my time reading all of them. I had dreams about post-apocalyptic scenarios where everyone except me died. I could just sit in the Library of Congress or the Bodleian and I would read everything. When I was done I would leave and enter the wasteland and be the King, the only holder of knowledge in the world with the library of Alexandria in my mind. I firmly believed I could transcend my body through pure information, like a square that realizes God is just a flat line, and the more I read and learned the more I added lines to myself. All I wanted was to try to discern what caused the galaxy to live, or to continue living, and if there was no secret, well, I would die trying to find it anyway. I invested in an MP3 player, I listened to books in the shower and in lectures given by my tutors who I was positive knew less than I did, I listened while walking or running (you can't read everything if you only live to forty), or with one bud in when I was talking to my godfather on the phone. I only didn't listen or read when I was asleep, and not for lack of trying. I wrote my thoughts in books; small notebooks at first but that became too expensive, so then into folders of papers. When I lacked the money at the end of the month my walls and the refuse from trash cans around my university became my paper. I didn't shower, shave, even eat or sleep more than was entirely necessary because who honestly has time when godliness is on the table? I felt as though there were moments were my mind would unravel, or I would find out the secret of the universe and become the black priest, leaving this world forever. I started to believe that there was no merit in real people. I couldn't learn anything about them that I couldn't read in a book.

However, by the time I graduated and my godfather was expected to foot the bill for my education it became a reality that I would have to support myself to continue this journey. So I thought, "If I am to gain the wisdom to transcend reality, why not become immortal too?"

So naturally I became a writer. I would go to fashionable parties, and tell the people there I was working on my second novel, and the immediate question was "anything I've heard of?" to which I would respond something about unless they like post-Wallacian post-realism or DeLillian ethics, or another term that I had created to identify my lacklustre generation of artists that was not "post-post modernism". Don't see this as an effort to identify ourselves before the historians did it for us. I just thought it was funny, and I am admittedly terrible at these things. Asking me to make small talk is like asking someone to fry an egg on a coffee spoon. It can be done, it just wont be comfortable.

Around this time, I was living in my godfather's cabin in the Rockies. I had gone there for peace, not finding it in the city, to finish my second book, a sprawling family epic about a young son whose drug addiction forces him to quit his dreams to be a filmmaker and the repercussions of running away to California where he realizes that he has spent the majority of his life as a closeted homosexual. The only issue was that I couldn't get him to California. So I took to combing my beard that didn't seem to go anywhere and drinking alcohol that I could neither afford nor enjoy. We sat, my manuscript and I, unchanged, until he came.

I am not one of those people who goes mad and does not realize it. I had felt this coming for years. It was as if a tiny bug in the side of my brain had finally succeeded at eating through the thin line of sanity keeping me from being a lab rat that only responded to electronic shocks or a dog that drooled at a bell being rung. When I came down for breakfast one morning he was sitting on the toilet, allowing his bowels to ease themselves quietly while reading the manuscript.

"It's sortta late for breakfast" he said to me, barely looking up.

"I like my sleep."

"Philip Roth writes one thousand hundred words e'ery morning before breakfast, on a bad day."

"Philip Roth is a hack" I muttered.

He dropped the manuscript on the floor. "The horror, a cry for the ages, — — — thinks Philip Roth is a hack. Someone call the Paris Review. Someone call Granta. Someone telephone immediately for the police."

I realized that, if I was truly to go insane, I might as well use him. As you can tell, humour isn't my strong suit, so I could use this man's thoughts on the world in my novel.

And so we worked together. He drank too much, but added things to my work I couldn't have even began to think of. A ship, full of the dead, on which all men will one day die but some sooner than others; three young men and a prostitute ride through the desert in search of the woman they consider to be the greatest poet of all time; a man who attempts to swim across his town suddenly ages and is forced to deal with the consequences; a young child is given a toy cement mixer and becomes obsessed with watching it spin even though it is made of wood and never will; a grandmother who forces her family into a death trap she cannot possibly understand. I began to reflect and refract the truths of our species, and for the first time in my life, felt that I was adding something to the form, doing my part to make whole a world that had been tossed into fragments, that had been forced into a cage and when asked what it wanted had repeated "I want only to die."

"I'm depressed. I can't write when I'm like this."

I told him to stop being a baby. "We all go through this at some time."

"If you're going to be rude, consider this my notice." He glared at me from his pit on the sofa.

"Again, you can't leave. Not until we're done."

He sighed and began to sit up. This was a slow and painstaking process for him, a man who could barely tie his own shoelaces without wheezing. He looked up at me. Something close to sadness crossed his face. "This probably isn't healthy for you."

"I recognize that."

My friend stood. "I'm getting a drink. I might as well be drunk for this."

As he arose from the couch, leaving an outline with enough room for a family of three to sleep in comfortably shoulder to shoulder, the phone rang. He didn't look. "That'll be our editor."

"My editor." I looked at my watch. It was too early for her. I went to the phone hanging by the door, an old dialup that my godfather could afford to replace but didn't. I'm not sure why. I imagined that it amused him. We weren't talking much at that point of my stay, comments had been made about people and places and things, on both sides, that didn't allow us to function normally in the godfather/godson relationship.

I picked up the phone. A dog barked somewhere in the distance. "Mmmyellow?"

My editor and I ran through the usual spoon-egg-frying small talk quickly (this was fairly tedious but couldn't be avoided). We both forced obviously fictitious interest in one another's non-literary lives, and then said "uh-huh, sure, oh good for you buddy." She would talk about her kids, her partner, and the children's real father briefly, basic details I had a vague image of but never really received a full picture, as if she sent me a piece of a photo once a month of her life and I was expected to put it all together. Boring, but not the most boring thing about her. She had this habit of starting every sentence with the phrase, "but, um" like she needed that extra millisecond to decide what she was going to say before even the most minor phrase. I realized, after sitting on the phone with her for more than a quarter of an hour, that she began every sentence like it was the punch line of a poor comedian's joke; but um, butum, buddum, buddum tiss, crashing symbols upon my ear that reminded me that the joke, whatever it was, was coming to an end. Hurry up please. It's time. Life's a cosmic joke, and no one is laughing but the man telling it, while my editor plays the drums.

But um,

But um,

But um.

She wanted to know how the book was going. She wanted a specific word count, along with a play-by-play analysis of the character developments and what I thought the themes were, what the selling point to bookshops would be. I reminded her that this wasn't English 101. She breathed heavily.

"But um, I'm going to be in your neck of the woods tonight. Jonathan has a book signing that I wanted to go to, so I think we should have dinner. But um, there's a good Italian that John took me to once…" or something of the sort,

I don't really remember. It was a long time ago. She went on to describe the bourgeois shithole that another writer I had only bothered to read the reviews of his works for had taken her to. She included the gnocchi in great detail, down to the texture and the maiden name of the waitress who served it to her. I agreed to dinner on the proviso that there would be a referendum on manuscript talk; she begrudgingly accepted my offer. The Strand and City Lights Books would have to settle for what they got.

I put down the phone and joined my friend in a drink.

"She wants to see us." I paused, and looked at the couch, him holding his drink up to his face so he would have to make the least amount of effort possible to get it on his lips. "Me."

"Yeah go on then. Leave me here. I'll die of boredom."

"Don't be so obtuse. Don't be such a maximalist."

Without words we moved outside, sipping on rum and grenadine and discussing where the very angry young man character in the novel would go. I was only wearing my underwear and so was he. The neighbours could think what they wanted. We let the sun shine down on our bodies, comforted in the freedom that came from living alone and unsupervised in a world that was so incessant on being together and supervising.

After my fourth drink, it became clear that the temple that is my body had finally recognized what I was putting into it. I fell asleep and let the sun reach the crevices of my figure that had previously been untouched.

I was forced awake by silence. I realized I was alone, well and truly, and was late. I felt my skin ripple underneath me as I got up, and looking down, saw the layers of peeling that had already begun from sunburn. I swore, and called out for some form of moisturizer for myself. No response. I offered my kingdom, and nothing. I walked into the house which had long since fallen into a deep darkness. Peering through the window outside, I saw myself in the reflection, a red animal fixated on my own base needs. My eyes stung with disgust, with loathing or perhaps even with tears. I looked at the clock on the wall, and realizing I was late, ran.

I don't remember much of the dinner. She was cold because I was late, then she told me off for my lack of a manuscript and began singing the praises of the other writer she was working with at the moment. I noticed my hand had began to peel already; unaware of the rest of the restaurant, I began pulling burnt skin off and dropping it under the table. I looked at the second layer; it was soft and wrinkled, it didn't push back against me like normal skin would. I moved to the second hand. Like an orange, the skin came off in one smooth motion, past the blonde hairs on my arm as it went past my sleeve.

"I have to go to the bathroom."

We looked at each other for a moment. I realized I had just interrupted her in the middle of a sentence.

"But, umm... Ok, sure."

I began to unbutton my shirt as I walked into the bathroom. Stripping down, I opened the swinging door, and looking to my right saw a boy at the urinal. We made eye contact for a moment then he zipped up and walked out. I looked at myself in the mirror. I was falling apart at my chest already. At first I was too hard on the shreds of skin. I ripped and tore, making it hard for my nail-less fingers to grasp onto the thin remnants of red membrane. I finally began to make progress when I took my time. I looked at my shoes, and saw the pile I was making at my feet.

Soon, my shoes were covered. I looked in the mirror, and saw on my shoulder one last trace of the burn. I peeled it off and saw what was underneath.

~o~

This piece was greatly inspired by three separate sources; *Frankenstein* by Mary Shelley, *The Black Monk* by Anton Chekhov, and *The Circular Ruins* by Jorge Luis Borges. I toyed for ages, while struggling to write myself, on what it would be like to create the perfect author for myself, the ideal assistant to fill all the gaps that stop the artist from producing. I realized that these three canonical writers had similar thoughts, and so I began to turn *Coffee Spoons* over in my mind. What really interests me about the piece is the narrator's reliance on other writers for his "brilliant" ideas and his confident attitude that is constantly undermined by his actions and his thoughts. References to earlier work are common here, as I feel that it adds an extra layer of depth to the story through the words of other writers. This is a story about the struggle to create that almost every writer can relate to, and the lengths we have to go in order to combat that. Ultimately, that is what I strive for in my work; the relatability that makes the reader feel as though he or she is not alone in their more private and strange moments. Generally, my inspirations tend to range from writers such as Eliot and Joyce to Nabokov all the way to David Foster Wallace and Don DeLillo, although right now I am going through an obsession with the Latin American Boom and Roberto Bolaño.

# JESSICA TREMLETT
## SOUP

Jessica is a twenty-two-year-old writer born in Portsmouth, South East England and is currently reading English Language and Literature. She realised her love for words when she appeared in BBC programme *Hard spell* at the age of twelve, and has since been writing pieces for music venues and creating blog content for a fashion company based in London, as well as being an ambassador for her local animal rescue.

The first time Ryuichi heard the voices was in the early hours of daybreak, having awoken him from dreams of steaming kitchens and the sound of rich laughter. The sky resembled a large black canvas with stars dotted all over, and a gentle breeze drifted through the house. Only the faint sound of the trees rustling outside his bedroom window could be heard.

He felt feverish, his back was itchy with sweat and his eyes were dry and sore. His older sister Koemi lay peacefully quiet like a porcelain doll next to him, contrasting with the loud and distinctive snores of his Grandmother in the next room.

Slowly, Ryuichi slid from his bed and crept towards the door. Despite his heavy frame, his yearning for food made him stealthy and swift. He pictured himself as a fierce tiger stalking an antelope, much like in the picture books they had at school. Sliding the door aside he tiptoed toward the kitchen, clutching his rumbling belly, thoughts of tempura and ginger pork dancing gleefully in his mind. Their house was small but practical; with long halls and paper thin walls. He liked to imagine they were living in a doll's house and that he and his family were tiny people, who owned tiny framed black and white photos and sat on miniature kitchen chairs.

He indulged in this idea for a moment; before continuing on his short journey down the hall. Ryuichi only very occasionally emerged from the fictional world he lived in, and whenever he did it frightened him so intensely that he would swiftly retreat, pretending no such place truly existed. He often wet the bed and sometimes it would take Grandmother at least an hour to entice him from the house. Although, he didn't mind the garden; he liked the cherry blossoms and the way the shadows swayed on the ground under the soft light of the spring sun, its rays like a warm embrace on his skin. It wasn't much like the one he remembered from home, but still lush with wildlife and soft grass.

One time, he had found a skull half buried by the corner of the house, its jaw contorted almost humorously. He studied it, every crevice and curve, the smooth head and hollow eye sockets. A small beetle was clambering inside amongst dead insects and dirt that had collected in the crevices. He poked and prodded the skull until its jaw suddenly snapped off, at which point he quickly dropped it back in its hole and covered it with dirt, running back into the house.

He had cried a lot those following nights; the skull and its contorted face had reminded him of a fear that he had suppressed in the depths of his sheltered mind, kept in a box that had violently unbolted.

He remembered it all in black and white but could not think why. He remembered the smell of scorched flesh and burning. The sound of thudding footsteps and the high-pitched frequency of a radio while his grandmother cried in the bathroom.

But most of all he remembers the deafening quiet. The screams and stench had suddenly given way to total silence, before the smell of sesame oil and miso soup had softly enveloped him. The sound of a wooden spoon clattered on the floor followed by his sister's voice softly calling to him, "It's alright, little Ryuichi, you are alright," appearing by his side and using his chubby arms to pull him out from under the bed and into the bright light, putting her lips to his stomach and blowing hard against his skin. He had giggled and kicked, pushing her head away.

# Soup

Checking for signs of life before heading towards the kitchen table top, Ryuichi used the weight of his heavy little legs to swing onto the counter. Reaching for the cupboard, he pulled both doors open revealing an assortment of treats that were normally saved for after school. Ryuichi pulled from the back his favourite biscuits and sat cross-legged on the counter.

He opened the box and munched happily on the little chocolate sticks, the crunch cut through the silence of the night as he studied the kitchen. There were black and white photos placed at the centre of each wall; his grandfather fishing on the docks on the right, on the left stood Grandmother and Grandfather laughing amongst a chaotic scene of suits and dresses on their wedding day. And in the centre opposite him, his mother and father stood in front of their restaurant on the day it opened. The word 'Soup' adorned the entrance above their heads, and they were smiling. His mother was a beautiful woman, not like the ladies in the magazines or the television with those big eyes and red lips and expensive dresses, but more in a squashy comforting way. With soft skin and a long beautiful hair that she would often let him play with while they talked about the world beyond the city. He recalled she always smelt like rose perfume when she hugged him, disparate to his father who always smelt like old books and cigarettes. He was stern, but wise, with kind eyes and a generous spirit. Ryuichi missed them sometimes but often decided not to think about it. He preferred to imagine that his parents were dragon warriors and living in the mountains as King and Queen of the Dragon people. He had drawn them like this many times, with enormous scaled wings soaring above the clouds, they even owned their own restaurant there, and his mother still cooked her famous Chilli Beef Ramen.

> Ryuichi was eating the brown rice left on the stove after dinner, when a voice softly called his name from across the room.
>
> In his panic he dropped the bowl and scrambled to put it back to its rightful place. He looked up expecting to see a stern face but there was none. The kitchen was quieter than ever, apart from the sound of his heart hammering against his chest. He scanned the room promptly before sliding down from the table top with a soft thud and creeping back down the hall. He noticed his grandmother's door was open and sheepishly glancing in; saw her sitting bolt upright looking straight at him, unblinking. The right side of her face was webbed and con-

torted peculiarly, her eye stained milky white. Her face didn't frighten Ryuichi; but the vacancy of that hollow eye bothered him sometimes. He liked to pretend it was a crystal ball, clouded with fortune, the source of Grandmother's wisdom. It amused him endlessly and eased the unusual feeling in his stomach when he studied her otherwise loving face.

"Why are you up?" Grandmother asked sternly, before suddenly looking worried "Are you ill?" Ryuichi shook his head and said nothing. She squinted at him curiously, before turning and fluffing the pillow behind her and settling back down, "Go to bed, Ryuichi." He nodded and ran straight to his room, burrowing into his blanket, and placing his little hands over his ears trying desperately to drown out the voices that were growing louder and louder, "Hibakusha! Hibakusha! Where is your voice Hibakusha? Where are your teeth? I bet your Grandmother wears them on her neck. Hibakusha! Freak! Monster!"

Koemi came home the next day crying hysterically; "I hate everyone!" she screamed, "It's not fair!" Grandmother stood at the stove holding her with one arm and stirring with the other. "I'm sorry," Grandmother whispered to her, stroking her hair. "He is a cruel boy, you deserve better." "I'll never *get* any better!" she screamed, "No one will want me; no boy will ever come near me with all these stupid ugly marks!" Ryuichi sat on the other side of the kitchen wall staring blankly at a beetle crawling up the door opposite him. He listened dejectedly to his sister's cries with his good ear, and scratched his hairless scalp. "That's simply not true," Grandmother scolded, " don't say that."

"She told him! Hitomi told him! That spiteful witch, the way he looked at me, he hates me!" She cried even harder, Ryuichi hated how her chest sounded when she breathed so heavily, like a tiny person was raking at her insides.

The voices in his head began to whisper again, "Ryuichi! You have to leave now!"

Koemi's crying began to bounce from wall to wall, surrounding him, pummelling his head from all angles. He began thumping at his temples with pinched fingers.

"Go with your Grandmother, I promise I will find you," the voices were getting louder and more explosive, taking on staccato speech in different tongues. The skull in the garden came to life in his head, singing hysterically "Hibakusha, Hibakusha, Hibakusha, monster, monster…" Ryuichi pulled his knees to his chest and began to rock, he remembered trying to call out for his parents but a searing pain in his chest and throat stifled his frantic cries into the void of screams. The world was raining black. A woman held her hand out toward him but her skin was red and bubbly and peeling away from her arm like a banana skin. He had backed away, horrified, before swiftly being swept away in a sea of people.

Someone was carrying him.

He had looked up over the ocean of heads and saw black smoke, the whole city was engulfed in angry flames and thousands were running over charred corpses, screaming for their loved ones.

He squeezed his eyes shut before looking down at his hands, realising his own skin was hanging from his elbow like a torn shirt.

"*Ryuichi!*" Ryuichi awoke on the floor of the hallway to the faces of his Grandmother and sister staring fearfully into his eyes. He smiled unfazed and reached for his sister's hair, tying it into a knot while she held his head in her lap.

"Do you think he's..?" she paused, tapping the side of her head, "Alright? You know..?"

Grandmother sighed, "I'll take him to the Doctor tomorrow, he hasn't been well for a while now." She lifted his little body and placed him over her shoulder; he hugged her neck and breathed in the familiar, soothing scent of milk and soy. She lowered him gently onto the bed and looked intently at him, the same face that carried him, that saved him, that fateful day.

"You must try not to tell anyone about what happened, if you can help it," Grandmother had told them on their first day of school. Koemi covered her arms and back with a large blue kimono, Ryuichi wore a wide brimmed hat that belonged to his grandfather, and was really far too big for him. It fell over his eyes and if anything probably drew more attention to him than he would have liked.

Within the first hour of class, a boy that had been sitting behind him whipped the hat off and exposed his face, revealing his secret.

He hadn't realised how unusual he looked before that first day of school, the taunts of the other children etched deeply into his mind. The weight of the shame that day branded on his little body was a sentence perhaps even worse than death, and in less than a few hours he became a pariah amongst those who he had hoped to be his friends.

Everyday after school he would go home and sit, staring into his Grandmothers long mirror, isolating himself, his fingers exploring the left side of his face. His eye was pulled out of shape and there were no eyebrows to form expression. It felt soft and textured under his fingers, sort of criss-crossed like a fisherman's net. It was getting harder to pretend he had wrestled a shark or fought with the world's fiercest samurai; steadily the imperfections on his face stopped being gallant battle scars and were reduced to nothing but imperfections that quarantined him from the rest of the world. Ryuichi gazed sadly at his own reflection, and his childlike, innocent heart swelled with resentment, want and loneliness.

There was a perfectly preserved brain in a green jar in the office and a skeleton complete with hinges and joints so it moved like a real body. Ryuichi played with the coloured abacus on the little table in front of him, lining up the beads with all the meticulousness a child could muster while Grandmother and the doctor talked in low voices behind him.

"Radiation sickness," and "trauma" floated in an out of conversation but he didn't really know what those words meant. He slid the beads along the wooden line and counted each.

"One, two, three…"

"The left side…"

"Four, five, six …"

"Long-term effects…"

"Seven, eight, nine…"

"Little chance of complete recovery…"

"Ten!"

After the doctors, he and Grandmother walked side by side under the glow of the evening sky, warm conversation passed between them but nothing remarkable was said. She talked about how she used to cycle from home to the river and catch insects by the industrial hall back in Hiroshima. She rode a bike everywhere and the city's backdrop consisted of magnificent mountains and bridges that you could see clear as day, when there was no smog or black smoke, named 'The City of Water' by its contented dwellers.

"Did you know that, Ryuichi?"

Ryuichi was focusing on a rather large rock he had found in his path and was kicking it aimlessly in front of him until it fell off a bridge into the stream below with a rather loud splash.

He paused for a moment before asking, "Am I sick?" matter-of-factly as he ran his palm along the banister of the steps that led them down to their little house. Grandmother paused. "A little bit, Ryuichi." "Is it in here?" He asked, poking at his temples with both hands. "You're a little bit ill," Grandmother said, "you need medicine and maybe to talk to some people who know all about brains so they can make you better." She smiled and took his hand, "What shall I make for us to eat when we get home?"

"Dumplings! Pancake rolls!"

Ryuichi lay flat on his back under the warm spring sun. He had carved a neat hole in the skin of a mango with his fingernail, and was squeezing the pulp and sucking the juice into his mouth. A dragonfly flew around his head; he watched it fly into the sun, closed his eyes and listened to the leaves rustle above him. An uguisi was singing softly somewhere and the smell of blossom hung delicately in the air. He was lying on a cloud; it was soft and delicate underneath him, he dreamed of home when it was a place of harmony and comfort. A familiar voice whispered gently in his ear, "Ryuichi," it said, as a pair of arms wrapped around his belly, and the smell of rose perfume surrounded him once again. His mother swathed his little body in the soft clouds, cradling him as they floated away toward the mountains, whispering a gentle lullaby in his ear.

~o~

My inspiration for the short fiction *Soup* comes from a hybrid of interests in Japanese culture and life in war zones. I wanted to explore the abhorrent discrimination against victims of the Hiroshima and Nagasaki bombings, who, despite having experienced such trauma, were isolated from their communities.

The story initially originated from the perspective of a young girl, specifically, Ryuichi's sister Koemi. Ryuichi however, then became the pivotal point of the story due to the unique perspective that only a very young child can have in the midst of such chaos and destruction. He tries to hide in the comfort of his own imagination and home cooking, something that is fundamental to his family life. His inability to process what happened to him and the need to stay innocent is a painful battle that he is forced to endure.

My interests generally lie in writing fiction; *Soup* was unlike my normal style of writing, because it is of course, based on very real events. I am now embarking on a children's series called *Thunderfoot* about a troll living in Sweden. I would love to bring the beauty and excitement of Scandinavian fairy-tale telling to children in the UK.

# IRAM AHMED
## THE CORES

Iram Ahmed is a twenty-year-old student from South Yorkshire, England and is currently reading Creative Writing and English Literature at York St John University. She runs her own blog page where she likes to reflect about her student lifestyle and share her own creative pieces of writing. She is an obsessive shoe-hoarder and a major photography fanatic.

Eli's armour had shred. A small speck of whitewashed skin that had never seen nor felt the fiery fuel of the sun had revealed itself. The spot of exposed skin grew warm much quicker than expected and slowly, painfully, began to burn. Eli clasped his hand over his arm to shade it but it was too late. The heat of the sun scorched a hole into the fragile membrane; he lifted his hand for a peek to find a charred, black crater crawling its way further and deeper towards his bones. He cradled his arm and fell to his knees in agony. The blood rose rapidly; red lava bubbled to the surface and scorched its way up his arm like a rattlesnake that whipped through hot sand.

All at once, his protective casing split and the torture commenced. Strings of arteries and veins were ripped from inside him. He keeled over as tears flooded in his grey-sky eyes, his armour melted off, and the bones of his arm were crumbled before him, as though a deadly acid had washed over him. He threw his head back for the last time and screamed with whatever he had left of his lungs: a cry that pierced into the whole city for a split second and then… he was gone.

On the evening of that same day, Ava walked down the deserted streets as the Air Report Drones read out a notice for all as they hovered in the dirty, dank streets at around eight feet high. These metal, spherical heads each carried a large camera lens, built right into their centre. Whenever their sensors indicated a Core standing nearby they would announce the latest news that they were programmed with. One approached Ava and in its monotone, death-like tone, stated –

*"The sun is at dangerous levels of heat rising up to seven degrees centigrade. Keep indoors during daylight hours. Protect yourself and your armour. The skin we now live in may be weak but we still have our hearts packing a punch with each beat!"*

Ava walked on. The sun had set long ago but after a death it took time for most Cores to leave the safety of their homes. *Home,* Ava scoffed to herself at the thought. The strong brick and cement are substituted for the temporary blackout, windowless huts that are now 'homes', the safest place one can stay at to keep away the dreaded light of day. As the air became too toxic, Mankind had to fend for itself. The radiation grew too much thus the revolutionized human was born with a shell of armour, casing the delicacy of their skin. Archaic terms dissolved and the more suitable title of 'Core' was established.

*"This is who we are now – The Cores."* Ava remembered the repeated phrase on Air Report Drones and Television sets headlining the news. The Cores had arrived yet society simply wasn't ready for it. The transitioning stage was here and death had no time to wait for the Cores to understand or adjust to their new forms.

That didn't stop Ava, not tonight. She had to see it, the spot where Eli fell. Some Cores wept for him, others cursed him for his idiocy and her argument with Tam suddenly flooded back to her.

'Nobody is careless with their armour, Ava…' Tam had told her, '…unless,' he stopped talking, re-affixed his glasses and looked away.

'Unless what, Tam?' she said through gritted teeth already knowing what he was going to say. Tam looked back at her, the green flecks in his eyes pierced through his frames, staring straight into the blue in Ava's.

'You know what,' he said softly.

'He didn't do *that* Tam!'

'I'm sorry, I didn't mean - '

'I know exactly what you meant.' She placed supplies into an old leather backpack; a news-a-gram, an apple, a bottled flask and penknife, each thing carelessly thrown in one thing after the other.

'It just takes one cut, Tam,' Ava continued without making any eye contact, 'just one, teeny, tiny bit of sliced skin and any Core would be a goner, would bleed to death.'

'Ava - '

'So *why*, Tam,' she wasn't going to be interrupted, 'would he kill himself by…b…burn…by, by doing it like that?'

'Ava - '

'No!' Her voice broke and tears simmered on the line of her lower lashes. 'I know what you're going to say and you can't turn this around and say that he did it on purpose.' She continued fussing over the things she was packing.

'Ava! Stop!' Tam grabbed hold of Ava's wrist and her backpack clattered to the floor. She could feel the rough casing of his armour over his hand against her own.

She glared up at Tam through a blurred barrier. She wouldn't let the tears fall. Not now. It should be him breaking down to cry, the loss of his family still showed heavily on his face, his eyes shone a little lesser since that day and now with Eli gone too there was no light left in him at all. Tam, the only person Eli trusted, the only person *she* trusted and right then Ava didn't know whether he was fighting against her, or for her.

The noise of an old television set murmured in the background. News reports were on repeat. Announcements of Scientists making discoveries on the anatomy of the armour and breakthroughs regularly emerged on how to properly maintain it. The whole world cried in distress as they desperately tried to grapple with their new biological standard.

Tam still had hold of Ava's arm, his grip tightened as he pulled her closer towards him. He stared straight at her now, his best friends sister, the girl he promised Eli he would protect. The girl he promised himself he would protect. He knew Ava was better than this. Strands of her dark hair fell forward over the fair, smooth armour of her face and as though he was looking at a reflection in a mirror, Tam saw the empty shell she had now become. Her eyes glistened like wet glass and she looked down to the wrinkled leather at her feet with half its contents spilled on the floor. Tam followed her gaze and sighed.

'Where are you going at this time?' His voice was low and calm.

'I need to go and see it for myself.'

'Ava, I think you know - '

'Do you *really* want to know what I think?' The anger began to build up again, 'I think Eli would be ashamed to call you his friend right now.' She spat the words out wanting to hurt Tam as much as Eli's death had hurt her but as soon as she said it, regret washed over her. Tam's expression remained motionless but Ava felt the grip of his hand tighten on her wrist.

'Tam, let go,' Ava whispered as she attempted to wriggle her wrist free.

'I'm sorry,' he said and he slowly lowered her arm to her side and released his hold. Ava replaced the fallen items back into her bag, swung it over her shoulder and stalked out the door before Tam could do anything to stop her.

Now, here she was where everyone else had abandoned. The isolated outside and although no other Cores were out, the streets were still alive with moving billboards and pictures that danced rhythmically. The rubble from the buildings and the shattered glass from skyscrapers still remained in heaps out here in the streets. As Ava carried on through she noticed fresh flyers pasted on walls and doors. Some had diagrams of the scaly, armoured shell of an arm with annotations drawn from it indicating the different layers it consisted of. Others told us to '*Remain Calm*' to '*Fight on!*' Other's showed images of a golden sun, with raging flames drawn from it as it read 'Avoid daylight!' Another, on the windshield wiper of an abandoned car, read '*The skin we now live in may be weak but we still have our hearts -* ' Ava whipped this out from under the wiper and ripped it up in uneven, small squares, allowing the wind to carry it away into the debris. She could see straight through the government's attempts to restore order and steer away from the panic of the Transitioning. Ava heard the sound of an Air Report Drone speaking in the distance; *I'm not the only one out here? Finally, some Cores with courage*, she thought. She stopped for a second and looked around her. She couldn't see anyone and turned back around.

'Ah!' Ava stumbled back as a hologram ad stepped out of its frame and stood straight in front of her, blocking her way. It was an attractive spokes-core, with sharp features and a rigid, square jaw. His electric, blue aura trailed down the whole street, illuminating the darkness in the distance.

"Hi there," his voice was rehearsed, robotic, "*now does your armour need more care? Are you suffering from armour dryness and sensitivity? Then purchase the NEW Armour repair plan for just thirty gills a pack!*" Ava's hands curled into little fists and her body tensed.

"*Say YES for more d-ddd - *"

'Oh shove off!' Ava pushed the hologram with all the strength she had, as if it was a real Core stood in front of her. She fell straight through the garbled image and landed with a harsh knock on the ground. *That did not sound good*, she thought. The Spokes-Core quivered and rippled, a high frequency pitch rose from it but it very quickly re-adjusted itself. It remained unhurt and smiled sweetly at the position Ava was previously stood.

Ava didn't move. *Am I cut?* She was too afraid to look. The hologram sensed that there was no Core around anymore and leapt back into his frame taking his beautiful glow with him. Ava tried to adjust to the new darkness around her. As she remained lying there she thought of her fight with Tam; this is what it had led to, her dying too. Then she heard footsteps from behind her, they were small and quick, gradually getting closer.

'Ava?' a voice called.

'Mia! What in the world are you doing here? You were supposed to stay with Tam! Why isn't he looking after you?' Her little sister's head appeared over her. Eli's eyes stared straight into her through the soft, scaled shell over her face.

'Ava?' she said again in a strangled whisper, she loomed over Ava's current, unmoving position, 'what happened to you?'

'I fell, Mia.'

'Ha, I see that,' she remarked with a half-hearted chuckle.

'Yeah, clumsy or what?' she forced a giggle, but there was nothing funny about this at all, a clumsy Core was a dead Core. Everyone knew that.

'Mia?'

'Yeah?'

'How bad is it?'

Mia walked slowly to where Ava's legs were splayed on the damp, cold ground. Her left calf drowned in a shallow, dirty puddle. The armoured shell on her right leg was split straight down the middle, chopped like a block of wood. Her bare skin, as translucent and vulnerable as thinly sliced cucumber was exposed. Mia didn't say anything and from the silence. Ava knew just how bad it was.

'Mia, help me up,' she held an arm up in the air waiting for Mia to grab it, 'Mia c'mon I don't have much time, we have to go.'

'But Ava, your leg...'

Ava let the tears they had been held back for too long stream down her face leaving a dark trail over her armour where the tear tracks ran. She would only cry when she was angry, and right then she was only angry with herself. She propped herself up on her elbows to take a look at the damaged leg herself and she smiled. Smiled at her stupidity and then looked at Mia,

'We have to go *now*, I'm not going to be here much longer.' Ava looked back to her leg, her skin was cut. Bad.

Mia nodded.

Under Ava's fallen weight, Mia had shrunk slightly. Her right arm coiled tightly around Ava's waist and both of Ava's arms were wrapped around the tops of Mia's shoulders as she limped by her side. At the place where Eli fell, Mia lowered her big sister slowly to the ground. Ava winced as the grit of the ground chafed her bare skin. It was too late to get help; they had left the shattered broken shell of her leg behind, with no hope left for it. The blood from the cut ran, and it ran fast. A few yards in front of them, a bundle of clothes were heaped on the ground. Ava made out Eli's brown, leather jacket. As though she spoke to her telepathically, Mia walked slowly to the soggy pile and retrieved her brother's jacket. She walked back to where Ava sat and draped the jacket over her shoulders. Ava shivered at the sting that hit when it touched her, she couldn't feel the coldness of it, her body armour made sure of that but a vision of Eli melting inside it sickened her.

'Take it off me,' she whispered, and attempted to shrug it off her shoulders. Mia obeyed. 'I won't be needing it.' Ava said.

'What shall I do with it?' Mia asked.

'I don't know, I just didn't want some homeless Core to take it.' Ava shrugged. Mia put her arms through the damp sleeves of the jacket.

'What do you think?' She spun on the spot, placed her hands on the hips and began to pose in front of an invisible crowd of paparazzi. Ava laughed.

'It's a little big for me, don't you think?' Mia said after her shoot was over. She looked at her sister and there was another telepathic conversation, with a knowing smile they both shouted out together,

'Tam!' The two girls burst into fits of laughter; they both knew it would be the last one they had together, so why not make the most of it. With the jacket still on, Mia rested her head on Ava's shoulder. Her eyes occasionally shifted towards the red river running down Ava's leg.

'Why do you have to leave me as well?' she sighed.

Ava scoffed, 'Because I'm stupid.'

They sat in silence and stared at the place where their brother left the Earth, a white ashy substance laid there instead of him. Ava soon would follow suit and as she turned to her little sister and kissed her forehead she said to her, 'just make sure Tam looks after you.' Mia nodded as the last words she would ever hear her sister say was, 'Go back home.' With one last squeeze of her hand, Mia did as she was told. She left Ava, left her to die in the wild of the city.

Mia wrapped Eli's jacket closer towards her body, it was as though her brother and sister were there with her, walking her home safely. The night was clear and only through a shattered window or the reflection of a broken mirror did the ash of the dead decorate the world like confetti that fluttered in a parade. It was easier to imagine it as falling snow, white flakes that lay from time to time on the ground, blowing softly and freely in the air – an everlasting snow. Soon, Eli and Ava would fall like stardust. Mia inhaled the scent of the jacket and smiled, *Screw you Tam, I'm keeping this,* and the brown leather held her with the intention of never letting her go.

Iram Ahmed

A flyer fluttered noiselessly in the quiet air and landed on the damp ground. It read:

> *The Transitioning:*
> *In remembrance of the Fallen Cores,*
> *Sacrificed to allow our legacy to soar.*

~o~

There have been numerous times where I have accidently cut myself and it's an injury so incredibly small like a paper cut or a stubbed toe and I remember saying to myself, 'Oh my God, that kills!' So, I took that to a literal level. What if something so small as a scratch could actually kill you? What if throughout human evolution, white blood cells have ceased to exist? Enter: The Cores - the downgraded version of the human race. As their toxic environment consists of extreme levels of radiation, bodies are weak and the human body has involuntarily adapted itself to its new environment in order to survive in this new world.

Through this transitioning process that is endured from Human to Core was where I wanted to retrieve a reaction from readers. I thought it would be interesting to play with the fact that this 'transition' could be a potential problem in the real world. It was issues in reality that inspired me such as global warming and I expanded upon it and reach a place where something such as global warming or toxic radiation has spiraled way out of control.

I've always loved the idea of a different world and being able to escape away from reality and submerge the reader (and myself) into an otherworldly setting. I have admired Margaret Atwood's *A Handmaid's Tale* and I am a huge fan of H.G. Wells with novels such as *The Time Machine* and *The War of the Worlds*.

With a setting such as The Cores, there is so much left unexplained therefore possibly expanding it into a full novel may be the next step I take with it. I also enjoy writing for T.V too and adapting my own pieces for a potential T.V. drama series or short film are my next projects to work on.

# SÎAN ROWE
## THE BUTTERFLY THEORY

Sîan Rowe is a nineteen-year-old writer, originally from Portsmouth. Currently reading English Literature with Creative Writing at the University of East Anglia, she is working on a number of short stories and her first novel. Having always enjoyed reading, her interests range from the ancient classics to Gothic to Modern Fantasy, and elements of these have inspired her writing.

We are all butterflies. We are all bound initially by our naivety, our lust for life. Like tiny angels, we are fated to be ripped from our flight. Beauty and grace hide a short life and tragic end. At least, that's what someone once told me, in the quiet of the night, smoke unfurling from their lips. I still remember how mottled grey plumes collided with chilled air, fraught in winter, and framed a picture of the misguided determination that tripped our feet and barred our way. We were all fogged. Our cause was often obscured by untreated whims of passion, our intentions always faulted.

I can't imagine now, what they would say. Perhaps I simply daren't. They were only a sound anyway, only words formed by half-blurred lips and wild pinprick eyes. *Every decision has an impact*, they would breathe, *and every impact affects someone, in some way. It may seem completely irrelevant, even worthless to you. Yet to somebody else, it is that which draws their lines and fills their lungs. It is everything. Maybe that's why we're butterflies.* It was this sentiment that used to drive us forwards, spoken as it was by the idol of our existence; we were all banded together by this splash of conviction in the heavy waters of our inherent uncertainty. *Find the decision that will give you your impact*, I would be told, breathless with exultation. *Only then will you feel alive. Only then will you have your function. We are nothing without purpose.*

This is something that took me many years to believe, to learn, and even more to understand. And even now, as I stand in the middle of the Square, sweltering under the midday sun and with perspiration beading across my forehead, seeping into my hair, I don't think I can say I have fulfilled my "purpose". Or that I appreciated what I came to know, the information that *Derrin de Mont* once shared with me. That type of realisation, the recognition of wrongs committed out of blind hope, always comes around a decade too late.

On my left arm, directly above my uneven scar, I have an insect bite. It's red, swollen, irritated. I could find some kind of symbolism in that. Perhaps it reflects my current position, both in society and with myself – perhaps it represents the nature of my ego, supercilious, prone to inflammation, despised (these are things that I have been told, recently). Perhaps it is a physical manifestation of my dysfunction, my discomfort that I hold with myself for not sharing what I knew until time had slipped from my grasp and shattered. Or perhaps it is simply a bite, and attempting to attach a metaphorical meaning to such a thing would be an absurd endeavour. Not that it matters. In truth, I find veiled sentences so stale, so unnecessary when speaking. *Derrin* was fond of them, liked producing vague conundrums for us to solve, and insisted it would make our minds *stronger*. People are now more direct with their words towards me. Only last week, as I walked through this same Square, someone told me that I was "brave".

A slow, sluggish sigh escapes my mouth, puffing out onto my damp skin and folding itself into the dense heat of the air. So carefully, but quick, like needlework sewn by nimble fingers. My mother was a seamstress, and a very accomplished one at that. She embroidered me a blanket when I was young and I kept it with me wherever I went until—I don't know where it is now. For a long while it lay across my bed in the house on the border, but in the hurried move last month I did not have the opportunity to take it. And now it is lost, that last keepsake. Someone probably stole it away, to give to their own children or to sell, thinking that whoever owned it would no longer have a need for it. I doubt I'll see that blanket again.

I have been waiting almost an hour. In that time the crowds circling around the Square have steadily increased and for a fleeting second I believe I see a familiar face. I shift my position, hoping to be proven correct, that there is a *friend* among the people, only then they turn and I realise my mistake. I do not know those features, not those eyes or that brow or that nose. Perhaps the waiting, the expectation, is finally fretting away at my bones; for I have found that the minutes truly drag under the sun, crawling along the burning stone on scraped knees and bruised elbows, having little purpose except to frustrate and tire those who stand in earnest. Or those who stand solemn. Or those who stand afraid.

I do not stand with particular emotion, despite the weariness that tugs at my very being. I have passed through *that* threshold. Besides, it would not suit me to give a damn, not now. There isn't any chance left for that. Not a single one. The time I have ebbs away with each restless shuffle of the crowds and the sun climbs higher, reaching its pinnacle, baring its teeth. A finely dressed man steps up across the Square, standing aloft upon a stage, and begins to speak. *"Pleasant greetings to you all, having gathered upon this day—"*

I close my eyes. That is under my control, still. An intricate web patterns the inside of my eyelids, slender tendrils of blood tracing out eccentric complexities, only visible by the blinding rays of daytime. I am but a fly, caught in a web, only grander, more exotic. Though this one is not visible by night or day – it is more figurative in nature. Palpable not tangible. The fine man's voice breaks through: *"Here, on this hour, you shall be the revered witnesses—"*

My memories billow under the sails of my imagination, and I can see their faces once more. Many of their names, however, avoid my recognition – recollection allows for only the wisps of sounds, drawn out or cut short, and I can't be sure of the syllables. Colours and shapes and abstractions merge, charged by the phantasmal disorders of my unconscious conscious. I cannot see what I remember. I cannot hear what I recall. Is that what I deserve? Some would say so – that's why I'm here.

I open my eyes. Life is flickering. Destined to forget, that is my place now. My actions are blurred, my decisions amplified only by the effects they once had – that which they once exposed. I believe that in some way I did change the world. A shame it was collateral damage. I can't take that as my purpose. *"Let it be done, in this moment."*

A movement captures my attention, and I glance to the side. I shake my head at the woman who approaches me, hands held out with an offering. She raises her eyebrows, expression twitching, but relents. The fabric drops. There is no flutter in its fall. Is that how it shall go?

I stand tall. They call my name. As I step forwards, I think I see a butterfly and a smile lifts the edges of my lips.

The irony is not lost on me as the executioner swings his sword at my neck.

~o~

*The Butterfly Theory* is a piece of stark realism that's concept stemmed from Edward Lorenz's notion of *The Butterfly Effect*. Within chaos theory, the butterfly effect is "the sensitive dependence on initial conditions in which a small change in one state of a deterministic nonlinear system can result in large differences in a later state". The metaphorical example given to explain this is the idea that a hurricane could have been influenced by minor perturbations, such as the flapping of a butterfly's wings several weeks earlier. This theory is lightly referred to in my story when the narrator reflects upon things they had been told previous to the beginning of the narrative. The theory is presented through the notion of decisions and impacts, as well as the way in which humans are likened to butterflies (in the chaotic 'hurricane' of existence).

The writing style of *The Butterfly Theory* was partly inspired by the works of Clare Wigfall, specifically her collection *The Loudest Sound and Nothing*; the sentence structure in her story *Slow Billows the Smoke* particularly interests me, as does the way she portrays present and past events. Other writers that have inspired me include Edgar Allan Poe, Daphne du Maurier, Shakespeare, and Virgil.

I find that writing is a form of escapism and allows for a freeing of the mind, a self-expression that can only be achieved through this creative experience.

My ambition is to finish a book of short stories, using *The Butterfly Theory* as a starting point – it is likely that a common "theme" throughout each story will be the employment of an ambiguous narrator.

# MELISSA WELLIVER
## THE WAR LETTERS

Melissa Welliver is a twenty-five-year-old writer, originally from Whaley Bridge, in High Peak Derbyshire. Having completed a BA in English and History at Leeds University and a MA in Creative Writing from the University of Manchester, she is currently working on a Young Adult novel and has previously completed NaNoWriMo 2014. She also runs her own technology business, and enjoys blogging and attending Literature Festivals.

**1. Frank**

Frank pulled the canvas back pack onto his blistered shoulders. The white sun was still high in the sky, thickening the air around him until walking felt like wading through water. The shining damselflies struggled to swim in the air, swaying around the men as they marched. Frank pulled his soaked shirt away from his sticky skin and tried to not think about the thirst that currently sat in his parched throat. He looked ahead and noticed that soon they would be back in the canopy of the forest, protected from the sun.

 At that moment a new sound appeared in the orchestra of forest noises. It was louder than the hum of Japanese hornets hunting out their prey; it whirred faster than the struggling damselflies and silenced even the loudest macaques' scream as they swung fast through the high teak trees.

"Get down! On the ground! We've got Abdul and Bessie, coming in low!" Lieutenant Vanguard called.

Frank's training immediately kicked in. He dropped down onto the earth and crawled into the tall grass that grew to the left of the track. Arthur's boots kicked up flecks of mud into Frank's face, forcing his eyes shut. He shuffled blindly forward, listening for Arthur's movements ahead. He felt the cool dew of the soggy grass blades tickling his face and felt safe enough to open his eyes.

Sure enough, the Lieutenant had been spot on. Now rolling onto his back so as to avoid the heavy pack pressing into his back, Frank looked up into the sky. Two Japanese Fighter Jets danced together in perfect harmony, wrapping each other up in a ribbon of smoke. Bessie twirled round and round like a ballerina, seducing the other plane and pulling it closer to its flank. Bessie and Abdul: dancing on the grave attempt of an Allied invasion.

Frank smiled for the first time in a long time. This was the longest rest they'd had in days. He was feeling so triumphant, in fact, that despite his thirst he decided he wanted a cigarette. Reaching into his top breast pocket, his fingers brushed the sodden, cardboard box of *Players*. He winced; the wet, pulpy packaging was not a good sign. Pulling the packet out of his pocket, he made a small prayer to God and reached inside to pull out a limp, damp cigarette. He squeezed the tip between his thumb and forefinger and watched as a stream of water ran down his hand. The cigarette was ruined, and judging from the state of this one the humidity had left no survivors. Frank sighed, dropped the waterlogged box into a nearby puddle and waited for the mechanised killing machines to pass them by.

## 2. Arthur

Arthur hopelessly wiped a bead of sweat from his shiny brow, and he could already feel the next wave of perspiration welling up on his skin. Lying here on his back, watching the fading trails of the fighter jets, Arthur's thoughts drifted back home to Scilly Banks. He thought about the shaggy fields peppered with hay bales in the summertime and how as young boys he and Frank had crept into Farmer Greg's fields before school to jump on them.

He thought about his fifteenth birthday, when he had broken his arm after falling off his bike and Frank had ridden him to Doctor Matthewson on his handlebars. Arthur raised his head to look at his old pal now, lying at the base of his feet.

Frank was currently wringing out what was left of a cigarette, which caused Arthur to start laughing. Frank always took everything in life so personally. It reminded Arthur of when he and Frank tried to sneak a pint from the Old Packhorse once. Lucy Cull had been on the bar, and she had always had a sweet spot for Frank so they thought she could wrangle a free one for them, but at the last minute the landlady had seen them and given both Frank and Arthur such a clip round the ear. Sat outside in the pouring rain after being barred, Frank had moaned that nothing ever went his way and that his life was just a series of disasters.

Arthur rolled his eyes at the memory. All the girls fancied Frank. He was the handsome one, with his jutting chin and long eyelashes. Frank's parents were both still alive and well, and Frank had never wanted for anything growing up. Yet he still complained. Arthur knew that he had hit most of the branches whilst falling out of the ugly tree; he remembered how unfair it felt when his father passed away and he was never as clever as Frank at school. But Arthur understood that he was the lucky one. He had Frank, clever and handsome Frank, to help him along through life. Frank had even introduced him to his sweetheart back home, and Arthur's Mum had tried her very best to provide for her son. So whilst Frank was forever irritable and fussing about the state of their 'boring' lives, Arthur was counting his blessings. Even now, he was here in an exotic rainforest, surrounded by friends new and old, having one last adventure before settling down to his married life back home.

Violet. His lovely Violet. Arthur didn't allow himself to think of her too much; it made his heart heavy and his feet feel like lead. He couldn't believe his luck the day Violet agreed to let him court her. As far as Arthur was concerned, she was the prettiest girl in the village. They had all gone to school together, he and Frank and Violet. Arthur remembered seeing her on the first day of infants. They were five, and Violet had her hair in two long plaits with a purple ribbon in each one; a violet ribbon. Her pinafore was spotlessly clean and crisp: it looked stiff and itchy, and Violet had been scratching under her collar the whole time she waited in the playground. Arthur thought she was the loveliest thing he had ever seen in his short life. After that, he got to school early and waited for her every day.

He didn't talk to her, of course. Arthur didn't talk to anyone much until he met Frank. In those first few months at school, Arthur got into some trouble with the bigger children. They knew that his father had just died, and they didn't let him forget it. One boy, Ginger Kilkenny called him a 'bastard'; he obviously didn't know what it actually meant, but it fit well enough from what he understood. Ginger Kilkenny was a mean boy and he looked it: with his shock of red hair, piercing blue eyes and huge arms he intimidated all the other children in the playground. His Dad was the village blacksmith, and from the look of the burns on Ginger's arms the boy had been on the receiving end of his Dad's soldering equipment more than once. One day before school, when Arthur was waiting for Violet, Ginger and some of his stupid friends approached Arthur.

Arthur had known that he should be afraid, that Ginger would knock his nose out of joint with one punch, but he didn't run. He was too frightened. Rooted to the spot by his useless legs, he scrunched his eyes up tight and waited for the pain that was to come. Even now, watching bomber planes pass over his head, Arthur had never been as scared in his life as when he had seen Ginger Kilkenny coming across that playground.

But the pain never came. After a few minutes, Arthur had sneaked a peak through his stubby eyelashes, looking for his assailant. When he clocked Ginger lying on the playground in a pool of his own blood, Arthur's eyes had shot wide open like saucers. Standing over Ginger, being held back by Mrs Harding, the reception teacher, was Frank. His fists were still swinging, stained with Ginger's blood. Arthur couldn't believe that Frank had saved his life; because that's how it had felt. Just before the Headmaster carried Frank back into the building, the young boy looked at Arthur and he winked. From then on, Arthur knew that he would do anything for Frank, and Frank for him. They were friends for life.

With this in mind, Arthur laid his head back down on the cool grass and waited for Vanguard to give them the all clear. He would enjoy this moment for the rest it provided, not for the threat it posed to their very existence. That's just the way Arthur was.

## 3. Cowan

The General's bamboo hut was wallpapered floor to ceiling with photographs of beautiful women; women from *Players* magazine; women he'd known at Oxford; women from the cabaret here in Imphal. He was followed by the eyes of a thousand women, judging his every decision. Each and every photo was a reincarnation of Emilia, and each spoke with her familiar, condescending tone. *They should have been back hours ago. Were you even paying attention? How much have you had to drink today?* He returned his attention to the paper on the desk. *Dear Emilia*. He tapped the page with his pen, wishing that somehow the ink would magically arrange itself into the right thing to say. To his left a photograph of Emilia stood erect in its frame, watching him cautiously.

He picked up the picture. Her expression was stern as always and she sat in the acceptable fashion, one ankle crossed behind the other, her shoes just visible under the lace trimmings of her Sunday dress. General Cowan remembered, so vividly, the day the photograph was taken. Even the sepia tinge couldn't make him forget the awful marigold yellow of that dress. Emilia's mother had bought it as an engagement present: he remembered her trying it on and coming down the grand staircase, dressed head-to-toe in sunshine yellow and the way that her hand had delicately stroked the oak banister whilst she had held herself bolt upright, as if she was balancing a water-trough on her head. She had looked so incredibly graceful and striking that for a moment Cowan had imagined her as a faerie queen, dressed in dandelions and floating down the hallway and back into the drawing room. He had thought he was the luckiest man in the world.

That was before they were married. Before she had grown tired of him and his dinner parties; before she had taken to spending all day in the gazebo at the end of the east gardens, looking longingly across the lake as if begging the wind to come and save her. She missed her life in the colonies, he knew that, but instead of helping her he had chosen to gamble and drink her dowry away. If she was his Titania, he had clipped her faerie wings a long time ago. She felt trapped in his house. Maybe she had known the moment she had received that dress; maybe that was when her smile had faded forever. He couldn't even remember.

He pinched the bridge of his nose hard between his thumb and forefinger and tried not to think about the pile of unopened letters in his drawer. He squeezed his eyes shut in the hope of shaking the image from his mind, but found it was impossible. He slid open the drawer of his desk and stared at the letters sat stubbornly inside, waiting to be read. He reached for the topmost envelope, his index finger caressing the curl of the C in 'Cowan'. Emilia hadn't put his first name in the address. She was the only one in this post-war world that knew his true identity; his family's secret shame.

"Sir, they're back! The Lieutenant needs to speak with you urgently."

Cowan's second in command, Harris, had appeared. Cowan did not turn round to face the captain, instead choosing to keep tracing the 'C'. His finger copied the crescent moon shape over and over again.

"Sir? They need you. Shall I tell them you're busy?"

With that, General Cowan's finger stopped dead. He abruptly closed the drawer and picked up the piece of paper from his desk.

"No, Harris. I'm quite ready. And do me a favour, would you? Get rid of this rubbish, there's a good fellow."

## 4. Emilia

July 5th 1942

Dearest Klaus,

I trust you are well? And I can only trust, of course. You're silence offers no reassurances, and I have only the English papers to provide any information. But I still write, as I am certain that if you had died, I would have at least had a telegram telling me so. Even your death would give me some news.

It is not that I am angry as such: rather I am frustrated. I know that our marriage has not been perfect, but surely if any good is to come out of this war it is to illustrate the importance of never giving up. All around me, people are reconciling their differences and pulling together for the war effort. Mrs Goth has started a knitting club for all the society women which even Nancy Jessop attends, despite that nasty business over the village decorations some years back.

After waiting months for a response from you, Jane suggested that I take my mind off the war in Burma and concentrate on the one here at home. When I venture into the village with Mavis, I see them: the men with missing limbs, missing skin, missing memories.

At first, it was ghastly: it made me realise for the first time that it was not only me that had been affected by this war. When I returned to our large, empty home one evening I realised that there was something I could do for the war effort – something that could help not only the injured sons and brothers of the village but could also help myself.

I have decided to turn our home into a rehabilitation centre for injured soldiers. I say I, but Jane should really take all the credit, as she is the one with medical training. She has been volunteering as a nurse for the Red Cross, and was able to put me in touch with all the right people. It has afforded the opportunity to do some good and once again the house is filled with noise. It is just like when we first got married, but also entirely different – the conversation still centres around politics and culture, but these conversations cross class thresholds. Just the other day, I overheard Private Williams talking with Sergeant Kelp about the merits of the Futurist Manifesto. Imagine! A Private and a senior officer, chatting avidly about foreign politics. And do you remember Henry Jenkins? The lawyer's son that inherited Mr Lomas's estate? He's ended up here too. Nothing too serious, just a small shrapnel wound to the knee and he's hoping to be redeployed before the war is through.

Anyway, it turns out that he is the most talented painter. One morning soon after he arrived I found him sat on the edge of his bed struggling into his dressing gown, trying to manoeuvre himself into his wheelchair. When I asked him what he was doing, he said he needed to collect some personal effects from his house right away. After a few minutes of arguing, he calmed down enough to confide in me that he was an artist, and felt that having his paints near to him would speed along his recovery. As his estate is not too far, I arranged to have them picked up immediately.

Well, it has been the most marvellous medicine: Henry has turned the house into an art school. Once the other patients saw his work, they were as taken as I was. Henry has kindly started to teach the men and nurses alike to paint; Doctor Harrow calls it 'art therapy'. Henry really is a fascinating man; he often keeps me up talking long after my bed shift finishes. You and he are worlds apart, but I think you would like him.

It's the first time in my life I have felt important, and I'm not afraid to admit that to you now. I want to make this work, Nicklaus. The time apart has done me good – I have found my true calling. But this is a marriage of two halves. Please, please write me back soon. I miss you, darling.

Forever yours,

Emilia

## 5. Frank

As far as Frank was concerned, the constant marching was the worst bloody part of this war. He had been in Burma eight weeks now and hadn't seen another human face except those of the ruddy, mucky men. The mud on his own face had dried into a tight mask. He despised this jungle. He missed home; he missed sparrows and green fields and rain that was actually cold. Although if he did think of home, he thought of the shame and guilt he had left behind, feelings strong enough to push down the homesickness for a while.

Arthur shoved Frank's shoulder forward, stirring him from his thoughts. Frank turned and took in the familiar, grinning face; he could never resist smiling back at Arthur. His companion's excitable smile could cheer up even the meanest of men: his teeth jostled for position like soldiers marching shoulder-to-shoulder into battle. His eyes were sunken below a sea of crinkled skin, their jungle-green colour just visible in the late afternoon sun. Frank's mother would say that Arthur had a nose you could hang your coat on; it protruded out of his face and it reminded Frank of the beaks of the Chinese Francolins that regularly waddled alongside the platoon. No, Arthur wasn't a looker, but what he lacked in style he made up for in wit.

"Cheer up, old pal," sang the grinning loon, "now, have I ever told you about the time that I was ambushed by a group of three breasted Imphal women?"

Frank had heard the fantastic tale of the illusive three breasted women of Imphal. He had often wished he could see the three bosoms of these jungle beauties; he had often wondered if these women, had they been real, would have worked the local cabarets of which General Punch was so fond. He imagined the smell of tea leaves from the natural, woven necklaces that they had given to Arthur before taking him back to their huge bamboo and ivory tower in the deep jungle. Frank was blinded by the glare of its shiny surface, the brilliant white ivory reflecting the hot sun back into the depths of the forest. Yes, Frank had heard all of Arthur's balderdash before: sometimes he had entertained the idea that it might be true, but today he was not in the mood.

"Give it a rest, eh, Arthur? I chose not to walk behind the Elephants today because I *didn't* want to be sprayed with bullshit."

So as to illustrate his point, Frank pointed not one hundred yards ahead of them to the front of the platoon. There, so tall and wide that they blocked out the sun that was now dipping behind the Chocolate Step mountains, were four Indian Elephants. Their long trunks swayed back and forth with their heavy movement, their masters moving in faultless synchronisation with their gait. Each one was in perfect control of the heaving mass beneath them, able to change direction or halt with the smallest tug on the long reins. Frank always fancied that they looked like Indian princes, riding into battle on their leather thrones, high above the melee.

A roar of laughter followed Frank's jibe at his old friend: a sense of relief reigned after another day fraught with danger. Frank smiled, cracking his mud-mask, and turned to Arthur. He would have to hear another of Arthur's stories tomorrow, but that was fine by him; just as long as they were all still around to hear it. Frank gave Arthur a good-natured shove and the clumsy boy from Scilly Banks stumbled a few feet away from the platoon, still grinning his trademark smile.

And then he walked two steps forward, set off a land mine and exploded into a million fragments of flesh and memories and teeth.

## 6. Violet

5th July 1942

Dear Frank,

I hope that this letter finds you in good spirits. I am sorry it has taken me this long to work up the courage to write you. I wrote so many drafts of this letter, in which I blamed the postman for not receiving your letters or the war for making me too busy to reply, but neither is really true. For I did receive all your letters, Frank, I just didn't know what to say.

In answer to your question: yes. I think about that night all the time, the night before you and Arthur left. I think about everything you said and how warm your lips were against mine outside the Old Packhorse and how it made me feel. And I did feel, I mean really feel something, for the first time in a long time. It felt like someone had released a hundred tiny butterflies in my stomach; it felt like my knees were going to give way and my heart was going to burst.

But feelings like that don't last. I know that now. Since you've been gone, the feeling has too. At church last Sunday, the reverend gave a sermon about not succumbing to sin during these hard times. He concentrated mostly on lust, and how we should be supporting our men whether or not they are near to us. This seemed poignant to the congregation; it's mostly women there save for old Malcolm Langford, who of course was too elderly to go, and Mrs Faversham's son, who went blind in France and has been sent home indefinitely. The whole village is distinctly female now: they've had to close two of the taverns as they lost all their patrons to the war. In fact, the Old Packhorse is the W.I's new meeting place. I bet Arthur would hate that if he found out. I haven't told him yet. I haven't told him a lot of things.

That is why I am writing now. I love Arthur, I always did. I just didn't realise what I had until it was gone. He is the sweetest, most caring man in the whole village and I don't deserve him right now, but I'm going to try. When you both get back, I am going to be the best fiancé Scilly Banks has ever seen. The ladies in the W.I. are helping me make my wedding dress out of anything we can get our hands on during this rationing: people have donated curtains and even bedspreads, but I know Arthur will love it. I'm going to organise the wedding for your return, so it can be a double celebration – your homecoming and our wedding.

And that is why you simply cannot tell Arthur about that kiss. It would destroy him. It was a moment of weakness; a giving in to lustful sin. I love the bones of my Arthur and I will never betray him like that again. I don't want to break up your friendship either – you two have been inseparable since we were all at school, as I am sure you are now. He writes and tells me many fantastic stories of your bravery together, although I doubt one or two details (I'm sure that there weren't really 300 Japs, and the fact that you both fought them off with just a zippo lighter and a bamboo stick seems a slight exaggeration!).

I don't want one mistake to determine our whole lives. That is what this war has taught me: to value what's important, and to forget our mistakes. I just want things to go back to the way they were once this is all over, and I hope you can help make that happen. For Arthur.

Yours,
Violet


## 7. Cowan

Cowan's head had stayed firmly in his hands for twenty minutes. He could feel the sweat building between his hands and his face; the familiar, itchy sensation that usually drove him mad. He began to wonder if he could stay forever curled up in the foetal position in his chair, blocking out the noise of the wild rainforest and equally raucous men outside his hut.

It was these noises that brought him back to reality. He sat very still for a moment, weighing his options and trying to calm his breathing, but the shock was too strong – he needed a drink.

Cowan walked across to the cabinet at the far end of his hut and took out an unopened bottle of Tullamore. He rolled the bottle between his hands, savouring the gold of the liquid. Then he picked up a glass tumbler, which was upside down on the cabinet and, in doing so, he saw through the thick, magnifying base, a Bhamo Fighting Spider.

When he had learned that he would be deployed to Burma, General Cowan had got out every book he could find on the country and it's less sociable inhabitants: the deadly creatures of the dense jungle. Cowan remembered looking for nesting patterns in enclosed spaces such as tree trunks and trying to differentiate the round, white eggs sacs from those of the helpfully named yellow sac spider, which were infinitely more hazardous. Thinking now, he even remembered learning about how the silk of the Bhamo was stickier than most spiders', so that they could cleverly conceal their eggs in more unusual nesting spots, such as the waxy underside of jungle leaves. He recognised the blue patches down its back which shone in the light like an oil slick. It looked up at him through the glass with its two large front eyes giving it the impression of shock. The third and fourth eyes acted peripherally on the sides of the spider's head, looking out for any flanking threats. The thick pincers on its head looked furry and soft; although Cowan was sure he'd get a nasty bite if he tried to stroke them.

The arachnid wasn't as dangerous as it looked, however. Cowan remembered that it had a desire to kill every other male spider it came across, but was uninterested in any other animal – including humans. The General smiled; he always admired a good fighting spirit. This spider, however, would be the fiercest fighter of its species: it was a Mother. Along the bottom of the glass hung the row upon row of those sticky white eggs sacs; he guessed the only reason he could see them at all was because of the magnifying properties of the glass. But he could see them: he could see how symmetrical the spaces were between each egg and how perfectly round each sac was. The wonder of nature had taken him by surprise; despite living essentially in a jungle, the General rarely left his hut, constantly mapping out offenses and planning covert operations. Calm washed over him now as he left behind the events of the day to watch the thing; it reminded him of training, and the feeling of excitement and anticipation.

Cowan squinted and tried to count how many tiny fighters would be born from this one spider's platoon, but there were far too many. Lines of tiny, unborn soldiers lined up ready for battle. These were creatures born to fight, forced into a dangerous vocation in which there was no room for error. Anything but victory meant a quick death in the jungle.

He felt a sudden fury at the spider and her eggs. It was only a matter of time before her whole operation was rumbled; before a destructive man with a bitter temperament peered through the window and saw the sleeping soldiers lying in wait. Cowan picked up the tumbler and hurled it hard against the bamboo wall, watching it shatter into a thousand pieces of spider and glass.

~o~

The initial idea for this piece came from my more historical interests during the final year of my undergraduate degree. When browsing the archive files I came across a series of untitled photographs that had been donated to the library by someone only known as 'Cowan'. These photos had few details other than their subjects and the date at which they were taken, which was between 1940 and 1945 in Burma. I knew that my Grandad Frank had been deployed to Burma and it struck me that I knew little about the war from that part of the world. I set about collecting up photographs and letters from the time, some of which were sent by my great uncle, Arthur, and built up the characters from there. Although the characters themselves do not particularly fit their namesakes (I had next to no information on 'Cowan' at all) I used this mass of information to create each of my protagonists. I soon realised that writing about a war in Burma meant that I couldn't include many female characters, and I wanted some strong females to balance the testosterone. Seeing as most of my information was coming from pictures and letters, I decided that they were a good way to slot in the female characters without them feeling too intrusive to the story: hence the series of letters and stories were born. I decided to use mostly photographs and letters as my inspiration as there was something immensely personal about their perspective on the war in general. I utilised some of my own knowledge and text books in order to check some of the finer details – such as about the local wildlife or the codenames of the planes – but on the whole this is a piece of personal fiction rather than historical.

# KATIE LUMSDEN
## THREADS

Katie Lumsden is a twenty-two-year-old writer from London. She loves reading, writing and talking about books, and has just finished an MA in Creative Writing at Bath Spa University. When she's not reading Dickens novels or writing short stories, she also runs a literary blog and YouTube channel, called Books and Things. She has had work published in literary magazines such as *Brittle Star, Litro* and *Gold Dust,* and is currently working on a novel.

She says, "Well then."

And I say, "Yes."

We are silent.

We are sat at her kitchen table – or at least, I am sat at the table, perched on the very edge of a grey-blue dining chair, as though to remind us both that I won't be staying long. She is hovering by the side, back turned to me, watching the kettle boil. She takes two teabags from a metal jar and taps them into the teapot with a habitual movement, as though she does this so often she has forgotten she is doing it at all. The milk bottle comes out the fridge, the tea is poured – and then she turns round to look at me.

I am still not accustomed to her face. It is entirely the face I remember and entirely not. Her hair, once auburn, is greying, and her face is fuller, lined. She has lost that chiselled gaunt look she had when we were girls; her cheekbones are no longer as defined. She is less deadly thin, less unnervingly beautiful. The old rich green of her eyes has faded now. Yet still I can see her. A ghost of my old friend, a smudged stretched image of someone I once knew.

I wonder what she thinks of me.

It's a family kitchen. There are school newsletters stuck to the fridge with mismatching magnets, photographs blue-tacked to the walls – her with two children, with a man who must be her husband. The family grin and wave at me from beaches, playgrounds, country walks. I look away. The floor needs sweeping. There are crumbs and hairs in the cracks in the floorboards. Under the table lies a forgotten soft toy, a yellow rabbit whose ears look chewed. By the back door there is a jumble of wellies and crocs and muddy trainers. There's an open packet of hobnobs discarded on the side and the sink is home to a few unwashed dishes – not overflowing, not messy, but simply lived. Everything looks too domestic for her.

But of course I don't know her. I am mistaking her for another version of herself, a girl I knew twenty years ago.

"So how are you?" she says, as she pours the tea and sits down – not opposite me, but diagonally across, perhaps so that we don't have to look at one another. She places a flowery mug before me and wraps her hands round her own, which reads *Best Mum*. She is wearing a baggy jumper with sleeves so long they cover most of her hands. Her hair is cut short now, just down to her chin. Almost like my hair looked when we were fourteen and she chopped off my ponytail from behind. I cried when I got home.

I don't remember her as she is now. She is eternally sixteen in my mind, with long bright hair that stopped shy of her waist. I see her in a series of tight black dresses and different shades of lipstick, always trying to look older than she was. My memory of her is not of cheery *How are you?*s. It is of savage smiles and sarcastic comments, of that time someone complimented my dress, and she turned around grinning. *Oh yeah, that's 'cos I picked it out for her.* I remember her yanking on my hair, slipping her arm through mine, laughing as she blew smoke in my face.

"What have you been up to all these years?" she asks.

What have I been up to all these years?

I could tell her about my two years in and out of hospital after university.

I could tell her about the layout of our flat, the way it always smells of Emily's coffee, how the floor is always scattered with threads.

I could tell her about the way I've trained myself to concentrate, to keep my hands from shaking when I work.

I could tell her about the day I threw the phone at the wall when she cancelled on me for the last time – *Hey sweetie, I'm all tied up. I won't make tonight, okay? Sorry! Love ya.*

I could tell her about the day I got promoted, how I couldn't stop laughing on the tube home.

I could tell her about the day I met Emily, when my shaking hands wouldn't hold the mug right in the greenroom that first day, when tea cascaded from my hands to the floor and I thought I would sink down with it, float away in sobs – and then this beautiful woman, a few years older than me, got up from those silent glaring tables and helped me mop it up.

I could tell her all these things, these snapshots of my life.

But I just say, "I work in a theatre. I make and design costumes. And you? You look well. You've got two kids, I think Emily said?"

She nods as she swallows her tea, smiling this big cheesy grin that doesn't look right on her face. This domesticated wife and mother can't be that same girl who came home from her first term at university and told me she'd fucked ten men in ten weeks – she used that word, *fucked*, as though somehow it was her right to be crass because she was beautiful, while lesser mortals such as I must do our best to be sweet.

"Alice and Jamie," she says. "They're eight and six. And I work part-time in admin at their school – it's so nice. I love kids."

I nearly say, you used to hate them.

Instead, etiquette dictates that I ask something more about her children. So I ask about their school, their hobbies, their personalities. I listen to her keen smiley chatter, directed half at the wall and half at me, as though to speak all these things entirely to me would be insensitive, childless non-mother that I am, excluded from their happy little club. Her children are just as intelligent, well-behaved and talented as parents' children always are. And her husband is just as perfect, caring and brilliant as people always say, but never think, their husbands are.

"Bit of coincidence, isn't it?" she says. "I mean, that my husband's ended up working with your… partner." She lays a light emphasis on "partner", as though she is afraid of using the wrong word. She hesitates, drinks her tea, bites her lip. A sly smile falls over her face. "I always knew, you know," she says. "Always."

This remark both angers and inexplicably comforts me. So there we have it: her husband tells her I live with a woman and she thinks, *well, perhaps she was always in love with me.* Yet there is something pleasantly familiar in her vanity; she always did think everybody was in love with her. Finally, I've found a resemblance between this woman and that girl. Here is a string to tie them together, a thread to knot the past to the present.

And for a moment it's like I'm back there, sewn back up into my teenage skin. Like we're sitting in her bedroom, her on the bed, red lipstick, cigarette in her mouth, me in the chair, drinking tea, talking about nothing. Or at least, she's talking about nothing, and I'm laughing, because despite everything, no one in the world has ever made me laugh like she did, shocked, scared, thrilled, by the things she said. *Fuck those bitches at school. We're better than those losers.*

Only, we are not those girls anymore. We are two very different women, sat beside each other in a kitchen neither of us ever thought she'd have. I don't know what to say, so I just say, "Did you?" and she smiles.

"I can't believe it's been twenty years," she says. "It's like yesterday."

It's like a thousand years ago to me. I don't say that. It feels as though there ought to be a lot to say – twenty years' worth of conversation and questions, of catching up, of life – but I can't think of a single word. We seem to be done with that already. How are you? Yes, I'm fine, I'm alive, I have this job, I live with this person, I have/do not have children – and there you have it, a life on a plate. What else is there to say? We have told each other the bare outlines of our lives, and they are too different for us to want to look further.

She says, "Do you remember when we snuck out all night? We must have been, what, fifteen? We camped in the woods round the back of town and got drunk in our sleeping bags and slept beneath the trees. God, weren't we adventurous little sods? It's so weird, I was just thinking of that very night the other week – it popped into my mind for no reason – and then the next day, Ben says to me, oh, you'll never guess who my boss knows. Funny, isn't it?"

I think two things at once:

The first – I didn't want to get drunk. You made me get drunk, told me I'd be a baby, a pussy, if I didn't. You fell asleep and I stayed awake, lying shivering next to you for hours in the dark, thinking every small sound spelt death for us.

The second – the girl I used to know would never have used the word "popped". I popped round to the shops, it popped into my mind – it just doesn't sound like her.

Time is a strange thing.

"I can't believe I thought my parents didn't know. Like I thought if I opened the window after I'd smoked they just wouldn't realise. I mean now *I'm* a mum I can see how stupid I was being."

"I wouldn't have thought it," I say, almost without meaning to. It's only when she looks up at me expectantly that I even realise I've spoken. "When we were school," I say, "you always used to say you'd never have kids."

After her first heartbreak, some thirty-five-year-old (she was sixteen, had told him she was older), it was always, *Never getting married – screw all that. I want to be able to fuck whoever I like.*

Which I suppose she could, and perhaps did for a while, because she was beautiful then – no, not beautiful, but stunning, strange. She looked like a model, tall, thin, defined, unusual. Men and women stared at her in the street, and I felt half proud – I'm with this girl, she's my best friend – and half jealous, because no one ever looked at me.

Which she knew. She'd roll her eyes and say, *Don't wish for it – trust me love, it's a curse*, which was so much worse than if she'd said nothing at all.

"I guess not," this other version of her says. "But I was a mess when we were at school. I didn't have a clue. Isn't it funny?" she goes on, a small smile on her face. "You were always the more conventional one when we were kids. And now look at us!"

"Right."

"Oh I didn't mean it like that," she says, half stumbling – what's happened to her, my old friend, suddenly afraid of hurting people? "I just meant – well, you know, you wouldn't have guessed how our lives would turn out."

"No, I suppose not."

"You in touch with anybody else from school?"

Who would I be in touch with? We barred ourselves off from everybody else. I'd talk about going round to some other girl's house and she'd turn to me, laugh, and say, *Come on, we don't need those wankers.*

"No one at all," I say. "You?"

"Not one. Still, I wonder what happened to them all…" She sips her tea and starts to reel off a list of names I don't remember, wondering aloud what they're doing now, vaguely imagining marriages, careers and children. Twenty-something years ago she'd have made a joke of all this: *Which of our fucker classmates will go to prison first? Who's secretly gay?* (She never guessed me.) *Who'll turn out a druggie? Who'll be dead by forty?* I'd howl with guilty laughter at the messes she made up. And now she softly dreams up happy lives for our schoolmates with a vacant smile on her face.

She always did talk more than me. At least that hasn't changed.

Then, quite suddenly, trailing off in the middle of all this, she says, "Are you happy?"

I look up at her in surprise. "In general or right now?"

She laughs, not her old loud howling laugh, but a new, mellower sound. A motherly laugh. "Look at you!" she says, grinning. "You got snarky. I'm glad, you know. You were always such a wallflower when we were in school. Spent my life trying to get you out of your shell."

Is that what is was? Is that how she sees it?

"Well," she says, "are you happy – in general?"

I think for a few moments. I think of work, of Emily, of needles and threads. "Yes," I say. "I suppose I am." Then, "What about you?"

"I'd say so. The kids and Ben, you know. It's a good life." She raises her mug to her lips even though I can see it's empty. "I'm glad you're happy," she says, not looking at me. "Seriously, really, I am."

I was not in love with her – I was not so deceived. I knew she was hurting me, knew she half enjoyed it and half didn't realise. If she ever knew, I suppose she's forgotten now. But I had stitched myself to her, for better, for worse, sewn my shadow to hers so that no one could part us.

I had to break the stitches myself at twenty-one, when she found new, more entertaining friends, friends who'd smoke pot with her, who didn't blush when she talked about sex, friends who didn't order lemonade at the pub. Both she and I had had a tough time at school; I was quiet and she was different. I had always thought we were so close because she and I were both the same and not. I smashed the phone against the wall when I finally realised it was because I was the only friend she'd had.

I am a professional, but there are some stitches even I can't unpick without a tear.

It was all a long time ago now.

"Oh sugar," she says, looking up at the clock, "it's past three – I've got to get the kids from school." She's standing up, taking the mugs and teapot to the side, piling them into the sink. I slowly get up from my chair. "Sorry," she says, grabbing her bag from a corner. "I'm so rushed these days – I wish we'd had more time. We should do this again," she says, looking into her bag.

"We should," I say, knowing we shouldn't, knowing we won't.

I walk outside with her, through a hallway of children's coats and shoes, of crayon drawings blue-tacked to the walls. She used to strut. Now she shuffles hurriedly towards the door. Her car is in the driveway, mine parked across the street, but we stand for a moment outside her door. She opens her mouth to speak, and instead simply smiles.

"Well it's been lovely to catch up," she says.

I want to say, *you broke me*. You were my best friend and I was your pet and you tore me in two, bit by bit, day by day, not bringing me out of my shell but breaking me down until I was but a shell of myself. I had to build myself up from the inside, twist the fraying threads of myself into some coherent being, the one I have become, who you do not know, who you will never know. I want to say, no, it wasn't all your fault, and yes, you had no idea how messily my internal threads were crossed – so you didn't know, but nor did you care. I want to say, you were my trigger, my push off the cliff.

But that was all so long ago now. I only say, "It was nice to see you," and turn away.

~o~

When I write short stories, I tend to go through phases. In my first year at university I wrote a few stories about eccentric ten-year-olds, then several about people who had lost their spouses. For the last year or two, I have been writing and rewriting moments between people who have not seen each other for a while. Over my Creative Writing MA, I was working on a collection of interconnected short stories set in a café. *Threads* began nearly a year ago as a rough idea that I kept trying to slot into that project. I'd just read *Dear Thief* by Samantha Harvey, and I wanted to write something about the strange effects certain friendships can have on you, the ways in which individuals can be tied together. Partly inspired by *Dear Thief*, I wanted to write about a friendship that had been both treasured and damaging, about how that relationship might be seen in retrospect. But the story didn't quite fit in the book I was writing, and in the end I left it behind.

Only, I couldn't get these characters out of my head. So in October I started afresh. I shifted the tone and the situation. I kept the teacups, but now I sat them down in a suburban kitchen instead of a café, and I swapped anger for awkwardness, conflict for swallowed spite. I had the opening in my head for a while before the rest came: a mundane and ordinary greeting between two people whose relationship had been anything but mundane and ordinary. One of the things I love about writing in the first person is trying on new voices, inhabiting the mind of a character. With *Threads*, what I most enjoyed was exploring that gap between what people say and what they mean.

# FIONA MCCORMACK
## MONA LISA

Fiona Murphy McCormack is nineteen years old, originally from County Down, Northern Ireland. Currently reading English and Creative Writing at Glyndwr University, she has previously has had her poetry published. She also runs her own BookTube channel, and enjoys attending book signings and poetry readings.

*'Learn how to see. Realize that everything connects to everything else'*

- Leonardo Di Vinci

I sit behind glass inside a small frame. I listen to the facts of my life retold each day through strangers' mouths in foreign languages I shall never wrap my tongue around. Each day brings a thousand faces staring intensely from every angle, so captivated by my beauty I fear they shall go blind. Each day I am startled by a flash of technology and the instant photography which captures my image eternally. Six million each year pass through this gallery to see the portrait of a face forgotten by time. I am a faithful reflection of a subject without a history and this makes me feel as though I am an original creation of my own; independent of an artist interpretation because I outlived the legacies of those who formed me.

'It is thought that it took Leonardo Da Vinci six years to paint her,' the guide tells a crowd of gawking school girls who don't seem to be listening.

'Why's she got no eyebrows?' asks a young girl whose own brows seem thickly painted on.

She furrows them as though trying to spark some jealousy within me. I wish, for a moment, that I could express emotion. That my eyes could turn cold and my forehead could crease. That my mouth knew how to smile. But when you have lived as long as I have, there has to be some damage. My body is scarred with some imperfections from years of people searching through my truths and restoring mistakes they themselves created, and somewhere between my facial hair became singed.

'Da Vinci once said that art is never finished, only abandoned,' says a woman who spouts information about me for a living. She has probably said this quote from my creator at least six times a week but it doesn't sting any less to know I am an incomplete piece. 'He himself was a perfectionist so it is very likely that he never finished the portrait.'

Each evening, the room I have stared at so long becomes silent. The ceiling tiles which reveal the light of Paris above, slowly become dimmed until I am drenched in darkness. The other walls are cold and expressionless, bare from anything but specks of dirt missed by the cleaners who appear each morning to cleanse my quarters. I often wonder how an art museum could pick such an unenthusiastic, aesthetically dull colour and I wonder if it is only to accentuate my beauty. For hours I stare into the empty space, my eyes adjusting until I feel I am hallucinating, seeing part of a memory. Watching his concentrated eyes, with a brush in his hand, his strokes defining who I am and the oils becoming me until I am no longer the bare planks of wood he has called his canvas.

'Mia Signora,' he would mumble. Turning to his palette and stirring until a colour came which would bring him back.

I am woken from this reverie by a man that comes in to mop the wooden floor of my sunlit room. I wonder how the floor feels. And the water. And the bleach. I wonder if he is an artist as every so often he will rise from his work to look at me. I know someday he, like all of his predecessors, will leave. This is just his summer job and his future is out of this room and far from still paintings.

Soon the doors open to the line of people waiting to see me. I see small depictions of myself on some of their clothes.

'This is the Mona Lisa, Ivan. The most beautiful, the most famous portrait in the world,' an elderly man says to a boy, too young to be his son. I recognize his eyes. I imagine he's been here many times.

'It's so small,' the young boy sneers 'I thought it was going to be much bigger.'

The man stands aghast for a moment and it looks like he's trying to think of something to say.

'Yes, she is small. Isn't the detail wonderful?'

'Can we go to the gift shop please, Granddad?' the boy says.

'Her smile is beautiful isn't it?'

'This is bo-ring!' the boy says loudly.

The man sighs. He takes a long look at me and then decides to put his grandson out of misery.

'Fine. Let's go.'

The next in line is a young couple, their hands interlaced as though they are one entity. She is almost the age of my model; lost to the world's memory. She wears a beret and seems vastly unimpressed yet the man with large glasses is contented and they each speak an accent I've learnt to know as American.

'I think this painting is sort of overrated. I mean it's not even Da Vinci's greatest piece. It's just sort of blah. And saying your favourite piece of art is the Mona Lisa is like picking Shakespeare as your favorite playwright. It's just so… clichéd now. It's so Olive Garden.'

'I don't know. I think it's beautiful. And I like how even now people can argue over whether or not the eyes follow you round the room. Or wonder where in the world she is with the landscape like that behind her. Or even who the picture is of. Is it a woman? Is it Leonardo Di Vinci himself? If I'm not mistaken I read an article that said it could be a portrait of the artist as a woman. Either way, I like it. I like how everyone and their mother no matter their art history background can recognise it. So in a way it's like a universal painting,' the man says 'Do you think she's smiling?'

'You are so kitsch!' she laughs mockingly and they both leave.

Another tourist behind him rolls his eyes as though the pretention physically inflicts them.

'She was a revolutionary,' a tour guide says to a crowd of Japanese visitors 'Da Vinci was the founding father of the renaissance art movement and this was the pinnacle...'

Hours pass. Some marvel in awe and one woman weeps. Many take photographs of themselves beside me, their faces taking up more of the image than I do and it's as though their self-portraiture is more important.

A class of art students enter.

'Oh yeah this is a Leonardo Di Caprio painting, it's brilliant innit?' a boy at the back says.

Another sighs.

'So it's supposed to be smiling right?' one girl says moving around making sure that my eyes follow hers.

'That isn't a smile,' another girl giggles 'That's the face you do if you've got gas!'

'Ew! You're gross.'

'She was nothing special,' their teacher says, and I already know what is coming. If only I had ducts then the tears would come flooding through until my oils melted away my mere existence. I have heard this story so many times it is part of my being. And so I watch, remembering the glass between us is bulletproof and I cannot be hurt from such a distance.

'You see in 1911 this painting was stolen from the Louvre and wasn't found until two years later and the mystery of its disappearance is what gained public intrigue. Many people think that this painting is a fake. It's been stolen so many times that there are actually considered to be seven in existence. Now run along kids and tell your parents I'm a conspiracy theorist.'

I've been stolen. I have been lost. Some still stick to the suspicions of my past. And I worry that the rumors are true and I am the imposter they believe me to be. That my memories of the artist are just projections I've had thrust upon me from the brainwashing that comes with years of hanging on walls. Or that my creator was not Da Vinci. But if I am a lie, at least I have had the chance to indulge in the luxury of this life, for I know the world to be cruel outside the safety barriers. Maybe somewhere a beautiful maiden in a portrait has been vandalized when she deserves to be free and displayed for the world to see.

People come. They admire. They leave. Nothing is extraordinary. Each arguing over my smile or speaking of my beauty. Each bringing their own observations and rhetorical answers left and if only my lips would open I could tell them of my thoughts and opinions.

In the remains of the day an old couple are the last visitors.

'So what do we say Jackie, smiling or frowning?' the old man says swinging his arm around his wife's shoulder.

'Maybe he was trying to paint a smile but couldn't quite get the teeth right and he got upset and made it a sad face,' she says with a smile wider than the one I may have been set.

Tourists retort the smile or frown upon my face. Maybe the answer is not important and their question says more of them than it does of me. Perhaps I do not belong to my painter but to the public.

And I am left between loss and laughter.

~o~

I was inspired to write this short story after a professor of mine told us the story of how the Mona Lisa was stolen from the Louvre in 1911. This scandal is really what brought the painting into the public eye and there have been various accounts of vandalism since then. But many believe that the portrait which is famed today is fraudulent and that there are seven copies. While I was interested in the heist, and in Da Vinci himself, I wanted to tell *her* story. Mona Lisa is the most well remembered artwork of all time yet nobody knows exactly who the portrait is of and that woman is lost to history. I wasn't sure how exactly to tell the tale of Mona Lisa until I read Sylvia Plath's poem *Mirrors*, which is told from the perspective of a mirror. I decided rather than having the artist, the thief or even the subject of the painting I wanted the literal painting of Mona Lisa to tell the story for herself. The dialogue, I tried to convey as realistic both linguistically and intellectually of the people who visit the painting. Mona Lisa's inner monologue is not from the 1500s due partly because of the ambiguity of whether or not she is the original portrait and secondly because as she is observing visitors and the language they utilize is constantly evolving and so her language evolves with them as a universal reflection of her observers and her overall belonging to the public. The dramatic impact comes from Mona Lisa's internal reactions to the comments made of her. A running theme throughout the narrative is the emphasis on Mona Lisa's smile which is often debated about and to which there is no definitive answer however the story ends on the point that paintings along with the analytical insights audiences have of them belong to the admirer and not to the artist.

# EOIN WEST
## DEEP SPACE

Eoin West is a sixteen-year-old aspiring writer hailing from Brighton, England. While studying English, History, Geography and Biology at Bhasvic College, he is also working on his first novel. Having written numerous short stories in his time, he has won school based writing competitions and performed his work across Brighton & Hove.

Have you ever been less than one astronomical unit from the outermost tendrils of a nebular? Tea stains on the dark black cloth of eternity. Deep space is where they reside and where I find them. Riots of gaseous colour, the emotions incarnate in their grand fluid stillness, I am the one who stores the data on indescribable shapes and inklings. Sure the scanners pick up the few that aren't already mapped in this sector, long before you or I could ever see them outside the windows, but a scan can only tell you what something looks like; not what it sees.

I was brought into the universe and raised on this vessel, all I do is for the good of this ship and for the Union, nothing is extemporized on the U.N.S. Loeken, apart from what I do. My job is to record what the tech can't, it might be a few decades old, but I can tell you, it doesn't miss much. Even so, if the updates we receive every week are to be believed, the stuff they come up with in the research systems still can't replace me.

What is the message in a sunset, what does it invoke inside you or make you want to do, I don't know as all I've ever seen are stars. I've never got close enough for them to change from moth bites to hellfire. My assignment is to ask these sorts of questions, not some complicated position like navigating a course or regulating the hydroponics, but everyone agrees still much harder than their clearly instructed jobs. My telesthesia of the dance and reactions of the plasma clouds is something no digibrain can form. I look beyond the physics and see how they move, not why.

When man finally halted its selfish behaviour, the second Euro-Sino war ended, the planet healed as best it could, we finally realised what we had missed. Yes! We had traced out the seabed and named everything we had come across, but we had stopped dreaming. The blood and turmoil had blinded us, the heavens had been calling on us and they had a message - Why don't you paint?

I am the man who sees the nebular, writes about, photographs and scans them, so that the artists can get an insight only a firsthand perspective can give, yet not have to travel trillions of kilometers to gain it. After we set off from one nebular to the next, while we flit among the stars, I file my report and send it to the relay station at the top of the ship to be transmitted. In it is everything I can think to turn into recordings, about the nebular we had only just left behind, in the dark night that never ends.

"Igashu?" a young woman walked into Igashu's room, "Are you working? I thought you'd have signed off by now, you filed your report yesterday," she held a quizzical expression on her face, she wore flowing clothes like Igashu, but they had a sense of more knowledgeable feel about them, more straight lines and white or blue patterns. Igashu had more open clothes, flowing yes, but they expressed an attitude more aesthetic and romantic, greens crossed his chest.

"Oh, yeah I just thought," Igashu sighed, placing a stylus carefully down onto the desk, the rustle of fabric whispered, he turned around on his chair, so his two legs were either side of the backrest, "Look Emmett, I'm not really sure how to word this. Have you ever wished while making something that will become part of a higher thing, that you could instead make that higher thing itself? Do you read me?" Igashu stood up and moved the chair so he could lean back comfortably while looking at Emmett. He reflected her contorted face in his own, his eyes watched hers as she sat down on a pale chair opposite him.

"Yeah I read you," she said in a drowsy voice, "You know I just wish every cycle was downtime, since that last uptime I've been so tired, no matter how much I sleep I can't seem to shake it off." She watched Igashu stand up and walk over to a water dispenser, "Hey pass me a drink would you?"

"Okay," Igashu stood two cups under the spout and looked to his closest friend, "Emmett?"

"Yeah?" she had a slight hint of wariness in her voice, but the combination of the type of trust born from lifelong friendship and a general spent mood.

Igashu's posture slumped ever so slightly, but his words were still fraught with a fear that Emmett was still to consciously recognise, "Would you promise not to blab if I tell you something?"

"Sure, is it to do with what you were just talking about?" she looked out of the window at a trillion kilometers of pure emptiness, her mind dreaming of places she had never been, yet came from.

Igashu sighed, "I'm painting," the water stopped pouring into the cups with a hidden clunk of machinery.

Instantly awake, Emmett furrowed her brows and strode determined over to the desk, she gasped and looked in shock at Igashu. On the display was the outline of a nebula, the one they had just spent a week observing, colours were yet to be added, but the long strokes in different thicknesses exposed exactly what had been coming to pass.

For its purpose as an inspiration harvester, the U.N.S. Loeken required no art onboard, they noted down the visual lessons of the Gods crafted in space and then sent them on their way. To create something non-functional was to betray the very purpose of their existence.

"Look Emmett I never meant to step outside of my mission parameters, it just came to be," he walked over to her and handed her a cup in an unsure manner.

She received it with trembling hands and unseeing eyes. Igashu reached out to her, but Emmett flinched and backed away, dropping the cup, the water soaking into the floor.

'How could you?!' a rage burst out of her sealed lips and her gaze bore into him.

Igashu stepped back caught off guard, placing the cup carefully on the desk and reaching down for the one Emmett had dropped. He flinched as she drew her hand back as if to slap him, but instead she turned away and started to weep.

Forgetting the cup, Igashu placed his hand on Emmett's shoulder, "It's nothing wrong … I won't stop fulfilling my other…"

"You don't get it," she shook off his unquiet comfort and collapsed onto the floor, "I don't want to understand why, just stop okay?"

Soft tears brushed her unblemished cheeks. Her red lips faltered and then drew firm.

"I've never had to deal with so much, my discomfort and now *this*?!" She curled up into a ball and fell silent, however she continued to cry.

Igashu began to walk over to Emmett, when he saw how what he had said could be used in a way that made sense. He sat down to the desk, opened a new file and began to paint; the strokes of the stylus slowly formed a square like shape, then a round one in the middle, lines irradiated from the centre. He sat there working and looking. Every time he studied Emmett the water and biological chemicals dried some more, before long she was looking towards Igashu. The room was dry. Igashu brushed his hand in the air and Emmett saw herself before her, it was no mirror and the colour was off but it was the most beautiful thing she had ever seen. Her eyes flickered over the first piece of art, of imagination, she had ever witness during her life in the cold, hard corridors of her utilitarian abode.

Standing behind the shimmer of the hologram, Igashu couldn't see Emmett clearly, he walked towards her to explain when she too stood. The pair edged towards each other cautiously, the air full to the brim with a silent symphony, a reflection in the non-mirror. Emmett stood in the fall of electrons, eyes moist, looking, searching for what she felt in Igashu. The info-recorder opened his arms and mouth, "Emmett I can't explain why I do it," his voice trailed off as she wrapped her arms around him and softly, slowly, pressed her lips against his own.

Waiting for a strut to free up, this was a small supply station, the captain told the crew to head back to their quarters, until he gave the command to reassemble in the lockbay.

"I've never been in a station before," Igashu was lounging on their quarter's bed, it had been over a week since he and Emmett had officially announced their relationship and had applied to move in together. Emmett was laying beside Igashu, drifting between dozing and lazily reorganising her research files on a holodisplay.

"Do you think I'll meet other recorders?" Igashu asked the ceiling.

"I don't know," Emmett answered for it, she sighed quietly and turned over to place her head beside Igashu's, brushing the holodispaly away with a limp hand.

Over the intercom the captain's unsure and tense voice sounded out, "Assemble in the lockbay, repeat, assemble in the lockbay, we have been granted our request for strut access."

"Come on then Emms, we better head back."

"Oh I don't have the energy," she groaned and then smiled as Igashu pulled her off the bed and into his arms.

"How about now?" he kissed her.

"Just about," she smiled.

The corridor was packed with dozens of the crew walking, chatting and greeting those they had not met in a while. Everyone was heading towards the port quarter of the middle deck, where the lockbay was located. The ship was slowly drawn into dock with their designated strut by tugdrones, small metal bots covered in thrusters and suction pads. Once the lockbay came within a few hundred meters of the active site of the strut, cranes extended from the metal framework of both mechanical wonders and made the final delicate maneuvers, with what can only be described as robotic precision.

With the crew, from the childrearers to the 3Dprinter managers, gathered in the lockbay, a mixture of fear and unmasked, giddy anticipation materialised in the air. The captain, like the majority of the entire inhabitants of the U.N.S. Loeken, had never set foot off the ship and decided as the head of this motley band, to lead the expedition into the hospitable unknown.

Silence reigned in the black of space, unsubstantially lit by the light pollution from the station and ships, tugdrones and repairdrones filtered and glided between the outcrops of alloys and polywalls; information recorded by them constantly and instantly transmitted to the digibrain at the station's core, which analysed and crosscut every bit of data it processed at lightening speed.

The inner door of the airlock fell and sealed with a rush of air, the crew were now utterly cut off from the rest of the ship and the unseen station. Seconds passed and were lost for all eternity. Igashu breathed deeply and drew in the smell of his love's hair. The captain spun on his right heel and gave a reassuring smile that fooled no one, his lips quivered as they clamped shut and his eyes widened slightly in a defeated manner.

Shooting a bolt of energy through the mass, the white walls remaining motionless, unchanged, a clear cut voice, a sharp as a blade, rang out from concealed speakers: "You are now entering a U.N. controlled station, all regulations will be followed or your rights will be reduced. Have a safe visit," the recording ended and with an eerie low hum the outer door rose, steadily and with more confidence than the entire crew possessed collectively. The dulled glow of the airlock was supplanted by an aurora of polychromic streaks of dazzling light, sounds unlike many of them had heard for a very long time, if at all, slowly intensified.

Memories old and new materialised inside the crew's mind, before any could think them over properly the now forgotten door finished rising, not making a sound as it stopped relative to the tidal wave of flowing accents, voices, clangs, tones and everything else that flooded the airlock. The band drifted out onto the mid-deck of the station, this was where stalls, rooms and offices were located. The life of the station was here, everything a person could need to survive and a few odds more, such as illegal engine mods and robotic prostitutes, were housed, hung or sprawled in corners and under overhangs. The smells of spices, sweat and oil cleansed their sanitary nostrils.

The group splintered, with some enticed by a shady genmod stall, another by a literally eagle-eyed opportunist hawker, his implants fed by microtubes from a tank of biostabiliser to keep them alive, who swooped on two unsuspecting hydroponic technicians, offering them real meat kebabs. The Captain walked over to a decrepit and shamefully mistreated infopoint, blindly following his training regardless of the hall of wonders, illegal and strange, that pulled and grabbed him in.

"What do we do now?" Igashu questioned Emmett as the airlock door closed behind them, the thud of the edges resealing lost in the wail of a beggar woman wearing a Mandarin inscribed sombrero, who shuffled past a fire alarm panel. Emmett looked down from staring at the cavernously high ceiling above, flashing ads and teetering pods bolted dubiously onto the polywork, "Well the

Captain is sorting out the refueling and taking on board of supplies, so we're all on leave until the announcement on the intercom. I for one want to get a feel of how this place works, it's scientifically fascinating," she looked questioningly at her lover, who nodded in agreement.

"Let's start by finding someone to tell us where to go, hmm?"

A snake charmer's animal slipped past them, making Igashu jump and Emmett's blood run cold; the name of the profession was the only thing that had remained unchanged.

Damask curtains, great swathes of the stuff, neon emerald and turquoise mainly, synthetic, with small interwoven lines of pods filled with bioluminescent algae, was draped over the stall's carbon-bamboo framework. Conan Kalmár was a huge man, he barely squeezed underneath the canopy and each time he turned to face a new potential customer, his wares shifted with him ever so slightly. However, he was always too engrossed in his hawking to notice, and he had a habit of constantly stroking his short black goatee. He was doing these very things when the couple came across him.

"*Mask* sheets for sale, *Mask* sheets, five intercredits only, come and get them while they're bright…"

"Hello? I was wondering if you could give us some pointers on how this place is laid out, we're a bit new to it all."

The shifting mass of people, animals and objects healed itself of the path Igashu and Emmett had carved through it, before pushing the two into the green glow of Conan's stall in an instinctual last swipe. The grin on Conan's face was distorted by the eerie lighting of the cloth sellers abode. There was a distinct smell of brine and the sounds of the outside were muffled slightly. Nevertheless, all three still found it hard to make themselves heard over the crushing Indian Dubstep; emitting from some unknown, but most definitely close, location.

"Well what is it that you want?" Conan picked up an atomic egg timer and twirled it in between his fingers, "Say, you are two are from off station, no? We don't get many people from outside too often, not at least since the incident on Maroon 5, that was rock and roll - no mistake."

Igashu opened his mouth to speak, but before he could do so Conan had pressed a button on the egg timer's side which projected a cold beam of light over the couple, startling them. Conan tsked worriedly, shaking his head as he tapped the button again, the beam disappearing instantly.

"I'm afraid my dear," Conan spoke in a sollom tone, motioning to Emmett, "That you have a very rare, luckily noninfectious, sleeping virus."

"What?!" Emmett shouted, "That can't be right, no, no…"

She slowly sat down on a pile of worn red carpets as the news sank in, Conan slipped the timer into one of his multitude of pockets and presented a U.N. certificated doctor's badge, silencing any doubts. He passed the badge to Igashu, adding with a stern voice: "You do know this means, infectious or not, that I can't let you off station."

Igashu moved, angrily, slightly closer to Conan, but the merchant-doctor gave him a look that kept him in his place. Emmett remained motionless, her head curled into the musky folds of crimson. The info-recorder sat down next to her, extending an arm to comfort her and turning the badge over in his other hand.

"Is there a cure?" the waves of noise outside retreated and the music seemed die away; a solo artist screaming in a whisper to himself, guitar thrashing filling the position of backup singers.

Conan pressed his lips together, the cracks threatening to split open and offer forth their oozing rouge contents, "No," Conan announced as Emmett began to sob quietly, "Not on this station. I should know."

Igashu stopped turning the badge.

"What are the consequences of not curing it?"

"Well, I couldn't really say, but."

"Tell me," Igashu butted in, venom in his voice.

"Death," Conan sighed and turned to walk slowly to the back of the stall, "However I do have some meds that might delay the symptoms."

Igashu turned to his love, speaking softly in her ear, her eyelids opened wider and her stare into Igashu's black pupils hardened. He fell silent and she nodded. At the back of the stall Conan roared triumphantly, "I've found them and I can do you them for a real bargain." He was about to launch into a pointless sales pitch when he noticed that he was alone.

The couple's freedom glinted in Igashu's hand as they rushed, barging, their way through the crowds. On its front was an intricate painting of a nebular: their past, present and long future.

# Deep Space

~o~

*Deep Space* came from where most of my stories seem to come from, dreams and suddenly out of blue after staring at something for too long. For *Deep Space* it was also from a short story by one of the writers who inspired me the most to write SF and still does, Isaac Asimov, the story: *I'm in Marsport without Hilda*; from a book published in 1966. *Deep Space*, I feel, is about how, no matter what the circumstances, we are all human. It looks at art, technology, love and ignorance. Untreatable disease in an age of advanced technology is something that worries me now and I wanted to explore how it might look in the future.

Fictitious writing is pure imagination captured from the endless flow of life to be observed by one or all. It is an adaptable mirror on existence, which is something that excites me almost as much as existence itself. Writing a story is the only place I know where I can both record my knowledge, ideas and wishes while escaping from everything I know. As a writer I would like to create stories that people want to absorb, that make them think and dream - just like the best endless novels and spoken fables did to me. I want to share with the world those moments of bliss and understanding I have had from reading, where everything seems to make sense and everything is possible.

All the writing I produce is inspired by the work of many authors, including: Philip K. Dick, with his dark and hard-hitting worlds of mind-stoking possibilities. The comedic genius and limitless imagination of Terry Pratchett; *Discworld* is wonderful. And the incredible storytelling and captivating ideas of Philip Reeve, his Mortal Engines series changed how I saw literature.

# ANIKA RAJDEV
## THE EVOLUTION

Anika Rajdev is a Romance and YA writer and primary school teacher, from London, England. She read English with Creative Writing at Nottingham Trent University, and later on went on to complete her PGCE in Primary Education at Brunel University. One day, Anika hopes to write and publish a novel as well as a children's series. She also enjoys reading classics and spending time with her supportive family.

## 1996

Dear Alex,

My mum is making me write you this letter to say sorry for not letting you come to my birthday at the weekend. I am very sorry ~~but I didn't want any smelly boys there and we all no you r the smelliest~~.

Mum also said that I have to tell you we have cake if you want to come and have some, it's pink princess cake and it looks like Princess Jasmine from Aladdin.

She also said to come collect your goodie bag as she got one specialy for you…

From
Jasmine Daniels

---

Anika Rajdev

To Jasmine,
Mum sed to say thanks for the cake. It was very yummy ~~even it was pink and girlie! YUCK!~~

She also sed to say thanks for the goodie bag and the water gun inside it. I shall have fun spraying my sister.

I also have to let you come to my fifth birthday . It will be a wiches and wizards party and we will have a ~~majitian magican~~ magic man. You have to come in fancy dress or you cannot come!

Form
Alex R Marquis

---

Dear Alex,
Your birthday was so much fun, thanks for letting me come! I liked the magic man and the cake. It was very cool. But you didn't look like a wizard cause you didn't have the right hat.

Hope you liked your present my big brother chose it cause I don't no what boys like.

See you at school soon

From
Jasmine

**1999**

Jaz
Have you done the Maths? It's really boring and I don't wanna do it.
Alex

---

Alex
Stop sending me notes! And it was not boring it was really easy

---

Dear Mr. and Mrs. Daniels,
I would like to see you regarding your daughter's behaviour and participation in class and her communications with Alex Marquis. She has been caught note writing many times and it is not helping with her progress in class. Please can you reply back with a day and time convenient to you?

Yours Sincerely
Mr C Chaser

---

**2001**

To: Jasmine Daniels <princessjasmine@hotmail.com>
From: Alex Marquis <AlexMarquisthebest@gmail.com>
Subject: Chaser
What did Chaser say to your parents about your report?
Alex

---

To: Alex Marquis <AlexMarquisthebest@gmail.com>
From: Jasmine Daniels <princessjasmine@hotmail.com>
Subject: RE: Chaser
I don't know. I just got sent to my room and told that I wasn't allowed to see you for a while
Jasmine

---

To: Jasmine Daniels <princessjasmine@hotmail.com>
From: Alex Marquis <AlexMarquisthebest@gmail.com>
Subject: RE: Chaser
Least they don't know about our emails…LOL
Alex

---

To: Alex Marquis <AlexMarquisthebest@gmail.com>
From: Jasmine Daniels <princessjasmine@hotmail.com>
Subject: RE: Chaser
Please don't tell me that you just LOL'd…cringe! And Yep But Chaser has had it out for us since we were kids.
Jasmine

---

To: Jasmine Daniels <princessjasmine@hotmail.com>
From: Alex Marquis <AlexMarquisthebest@gmail.com>
Subject: RE: Chaser

LOL yes I did just LOL says the one who cringed!
Alex

---

To: Alex Marquis <AlexMarquisthebest@gmail.com>
From: Jasmine Daniels <princessjasmine@hotmail.com>
Subject: RE: Chaser
And cringe is acceptable…Tammy Newton says it.
Jasmine

---

To: Jasmine Daniels <princessjasmine@hotmail.com>
From: Alex Marquis <AlexMarquisthebest@gmail.com>
Subject: RE: Chaser
Oh well if Tammy Newton says it then it has to be the best thing since sliced bread!
Alex

---

To: Alex Marquis <AlexMarquisthebest@gmail.com>
From: Jasmine Daniels <princessjasmine@hotmail.com>
Subject: RE: Chaser
SHUT UP!

---

To: Alex Marquis <AlexMarquisthebest@gmail.com>
From: Jasmine Daniels <princessjasmine@hotmail.com>
Subject: RE: Chaser
And who says 'the best thing since sliced bread?'
Jasmine

---

To: Jasmine Daniels <princessjasmine@hotmail.com>
From: Alex Marquis <AlexMarquisthebest@gmail.com>
Subject: RE: Chaser
I don't know, my mum said it the other day about that new music player. Its pretty cool though, I hope I get one for Christmas
Alex

---

# The Evolution

To: Alex Marquis <AlexMarquisthebest@gmail.com>
From: Jasmine Daniels <princessjasmine@hotmail.com>
Subject: RE: Chaser
Yeah it is really cool. Michael got one for his birthday, I am so jealous!
Jasmine

---

## **2006**

<19:41> *Princess Jasmine is online*
<19:41> Princess Jasmine: OMG Michael gets everything!
<19:42> Alex_Marquis: What did he get now?
<19:42> Princess Jasmine: Mum and Dad got him a car!
<19:42> Alex_Marquis: Well he is 20 now!
<19:43> Princess Jasmine: So?
<19:43> Alex_Marquis: You're not even old enough to get your provisional
<19:44> Princess Jasmine: I will be in a month and a half
<19:45> Alex_Marquis: Exactly and then you will have to get take lessons and everything
<19:47> Princess Jasmine: Whatever…
<19:47> Alex_Marquis: You know it's true
<19:51> Alex_Marquis: Are we going to be immature now and blank me?
<19:54> Alex_Marquis: Okay fine then I won't tell you what I heard about Tammy Newton…
<19:54> Princess Jasmine: Wait what did you hear about her?!
<19:54> Alex_Marquis: Thought that would get you listening :P
<19:55> Princess Jasmine: Shut up…What did you hear?
<19:55> Alex_Marquis: Haha…I heard that she slept with John Cavendish AND Riley Anderson
<19:57> Princess Jasmine: OMG…NO WAY!! She's such a slag and she's only just turned 16!
<19:57> Alex_Marquis: And to think that you used to idolise her! Aha… SHAME!!
<19:58> Princess Jasmine: Shut Up! please don't remind me…that was a harsh time in my life

<19:58> Alex_Marquis: LOL
<20:02> Princess Jasmine: Wanna go to the cinema on Saturday?
<20:03> Alex_Marquis: Sure…What dya wanna see?
<20:03> Princess Jasmine: That new Anne Hathaway one's out? The Devil wears Gucci or something
<20:04> Alex_Marquis: NO WAY! That's a girls film! What about snakes on a plane?
<20:04> Princess Jasmine: Ewwwww
<20:04> Alex_Marquis: We could try and sneak into Borat?
<20:05> Princess Jasmine: But what if we get caught?
<20:05> Alex_Marquis: Goodie two shoes :P
<20:06> Princess Jasmine: AM NOT!
<20:06> Alex_Marquis: Are too
<20:06> Princess Jasmine: am not
<20:06> Princess Jasmine: am not
<20:07> Princess Jasmine: am not
<20:08> Alex_Marquis: Okay you're not…so Borat?
<20:09> Princess Jasmine: fine…

## 2008

From: Jasmine Daniels
(17:20) I cant believe we got caught! x
From: Alex Marquis
(17:25) I no! At least it isn't as bad as when we got caught sneaking into Borat x
From: Jasmine Daniels
(17:28) Yes it is! x
From: Alex Marquis
(17:31) How? x
From: Jasmine Daniels
(17:33) We got caught by ur sister making out! x
From: Alex Marquis
(17:37) So it wasn't like my parents walkd in x
From: Jasmine Daniels
(17:41) Oh god that would have been so much worse ☹ x

From: Alex Marquis
(17:50) Still on for tonight then? x
From: Jasmine Daniels
(17:51) ALEX!
From: Alex Marquis
(17:54) What?! x
From: Jasmine Daniels
(17:55) How can u be thinking bout tonight after what happened? x
From: Alex Marquis
(18:00) I miss u…? x
From: Jasmine Daniels
(18:03) Yeh right ur looking for a way of getting into my bed x
From: Alex Marquis
(18:07) Why would u think so little of me? x
From: Jasmine Daniels
(18:10) Cause I no u Mr Marquis x
From: Alex Marquis
(18:12) Oh reali? x
From: Jasmine Daniels
(18:14) Yup x

## **2010**

*Alex Marquis has written on your wall*
Congrats Jas for getting into Uni! Hope you have an amazing time and become the successful business woman I know you can be. I shall be waiting for you at home when you come back and I want to hear about all your stories and drunken nights ;) Miss you already xx

Like · Comment · Share · 5 minutes ago

*Jasmine Daniels has written on your wall*
Thanks Alex. Have fun with your apprenticeship and I shall see you at Christmas. Miss you too xx

Like · Comment · Share · Just Now

Anika Rajdev

## **2012**

Dear Alex,

Some friendships last years, others last days and some last forever. Clearly ours was meant to end at this point. After all these years you think you know me so well, but you don't. You think you can use me and then hang me out to dry, but you can't. I am fed up of your behaviour - you always put yourself first! It pains me to write this letter because you *were* one of my best friends, and I thought we would be together forever, but clearly not. I am glad I will never have to see you again as I am moving to Spain because I have been offered a job there as part of my degree. It is an amazing opportunity to work with one of the top firms there and it comes with a great salary.

   I wish you all the best for the future and I hope you had fun sleeping with Tammy Newton and that your future child doesn't get her looks! You will never hear from me again so consider this friendship over!

Yours sincerely
Jasmine Daniels

P.S. Do not even think about trying to find me or replying to this I never want to hear from you again!

~o~

My piece, *The Evolution*, was originally written in 2013 while in my second year of undergraduate study. This short story was inspired by Cecila Ahern's *Where Rainbows End*. I loved the progress of the book and how it wasn't just text like every other novel I was used to reading. I wanted to use that evolution of technology to portray the relationship of two characters and their relationship. I wanted to toy with the idea of having a romance undertone, so that the reader could predict what they thought was going to happen in their relationship. However when writing the ending I didn't know if I wanted a 'happily ever after' ending; I am an avid reader and I know that sometimes we all drift apart in the end. Therefore I decided to follow in the steps of my favourite authoress, Jodi Picoult, and put a twist at the end. I had previously mentioned the character Tammy and thought it would be great to incorporate her into a love affair to end their relationship.

However my main enjoyment about writing this piece was the influence of technology and how it has changed us. Not only did I have to look at the way the character communicated verbally, I had to also look at how their writing styles would have changed because of technology and their age. It was great fun to research and explore what was invented whilst I was growing up in order to make this seem a bit more realistic.

I really hope that readers enjoy reading this as much as I loved writing it!

# BRYONY PORTEOUS-SEBOUHIAN
## THE DRUDE

Bryony Porteous-Sebouhian is a twenty-one-year-old writer originally from Kingston Upon Hull in Northern England. Currently in her third year of English Literature and Creative Writing at York St John university. She is currently writing her first novel and has previously had poetry published in Anima Poetry's first journal and two of United Press' poetry anthologies. She runs her own writing blog on Wordpress and enjoys reading, drawing and finding new music to love.

*My children, I will say;*
*do not roam into the trees,*
*do not lead your brothers and sisters astray.*
*Do not follow the depravity of your parent's ways,*
*be good, and be kind.*
*Lest The Drude overshadow your days.*

It started with the Grays.

Their first born, Eli, was taken during the night. In a town as small as ours, isolated from the rest of the developing world, people didn't die often.

In Marantown, people didn't just disappear. But Eli Gray, he disappeared without anyone noticing. One week later, on the fifteenth of October, their eldest daughter, Mia went too. She had been a devout and dedicated young girl, known for picking flowers from near the forest at the edge of Marantown and handing them out to the elders.

When I grew up and finally had the courage to talk about that year - a year where our crops had suffered, the wind had been strong and something terrible came and plagued us with a sick enjoyment – my mother told me everything she knew, after speaking to the parents of the children who had been lost, speaking to our pastor, trying to find out what had happened. I wrote everything she told me down, not ever planning to let those words out of the small bundle of papers under my bed. But now, now I pass it on, too many years later to want to count. Now that I can.

Rebecca and Cyril found Mia's bed empty on the morning of the fifteenth, just like Eli's had been. And just like Eli's, her covers had been ripped, but there was no blood. No blood.

They took the bedding out, bundled it together, and with the rest of the town they burned the cursed things. I remember the smoke, even now, and how it smelt of death.

On the twenty-second day of October, their second son was taken. But this time, something was left behind. Rebecca opened the door to Jonathan's room, a small room that would appear like a large cupboard to anyone with more means, and she was confronted with the same devastation that had been plaguing her family for the past two weeks. Her pale face fell paler and her fragile hands began to tremble. The bedding, ripped, torn to shreds. Only this time, stricken with a furious rage at her children being picked away one by one, Rebecca Gray moved towards the feather covered sheets. She gripped onto some courage and ran her hands over the torn remnants, touching the space where her John had been. As her fingers dug into the sheets she began to feel something spiky, something amongst the feathers which had been strewn everywhere from the pillows that were ripped open like animals hanging in a slaughter house.

At first she couldn't see what was scratching against her palms, and then, something invaded her skin. A drop of red blood fled from her right index finger and began to stain the white cotton underneath. When she lifted her hand, she couldn't believe what she was seeing, and then she saw them, clinging onto the fabric and the feathers everywhere – white pine needles, sharp enough to carve through skin. Hundreds of them, and as she dug further down into the bedding, sobbing all the way, there were more, not just hundreds; hundreds of hundreds. They tore at her fingers smearing their tips with blood. *Where are they coming from?* Just when she thought she couldn't take it anymore, and as Cyril Gray was heading home for his morning break, she found the source. A hole had been made right in the centre of the duck feather mattress. A small hole, one that could easily have been missed unless you were really looking. But Rebecca *was* looking. Despite her already sore and wounded hand, she reached in. The needles ripped their way up her hand and her wrist, she winced, gritting her teeth and fought through the pain. Her fingers dug down, blood pouring from them, but she kept feeling on, a crazed determined look burning from her eyes. *There,* she said to herself, and she felt something, something cool and hard, buried deep down in her son's mattress. She grasped it with three of her fingers and pulled it out up through the hole with a flood of pain that made her scream as her hand came out. Her hands were completely covered in blood, so much so that it looked as if her very skin was red. And as she lifted her hand up to see what had been left, by whatever had taken her children, she didn't stop screaming; she only cried out louder. And louder. The words, "John", "Jonathan" and then "John" again taking turns to fall from her lips.

Outside, Cyril Gray heard his wife's terrorized screams. He ran in through the door, up the stairs and into their son's room. He almost passed out at the sight. Their youngest, Roslyn in the corner of the room, crying and quivering to herself, as her mother stood in front of her, bloody and full of terrifying despair. Rebecca hadn't noticed Roslyn was there. At the sight of another empty bed and the rest of the chaos around him Cyril almost broke down, but still he moved towards his wife, as to calm her. Just as he was about to take her, he saw what she was holding. It was a doll. A doll made of straw and wood, painted with black and white, a doll that looked just like their son, Jonathan.

Soon after Jonathan Gray was taken speculation began spreading through Marantown like a host of swarming flies, and fear hung over every household it could find. Initially the people of our town supposed Jonathan was the first of the Gray children to have been replaced with a doll, but then the families remembered the previous two children and how there bedding had been burnt. Had there been little effigies in their bedding too? Promptly, the parents of other children, the elderly left on their own, and Pastor Watson were all questioning what had happened.

The first rabble broke out during a town meeting where three of the townsfolk had accused Cyril Gray of infidelity.

"Per'aps the children did saw him Pastor?"

"You can tell by the look in his eye that he aint a good man."

"Been off drinking nearly every night since this all 'appened."

"Always had a bad side to him, is what I says."

The crowd went on, and Cyril Gray was more and more enraged with every word spoken. He lurched from his seat and took Mr Normand, an elderly man, by the collar. The chaos erupted around them. I sat at the back with my mother, watching, my eyes fixed on Rebecca Gray; a wounded mother, only one child left to cling on to. And as her husband got dragged out of the church her face didn't break from its solemn expression once.

A month came and went after the third Gray child was taken. The adults of Marantown were anxious, though not obviously so. Most people had decided to believe that it was, after all, Cyril Gray who had killed his children in a guilt ridden frenzy for being disloyal to his family. A week after the second fight he had started in the town, Rebecca Gray and the rest of the town awoke one morning to find him gone, leaving only a note that read "Sorry, my dear Becca." And so people tried to forget, but we, the children didn't. The three Gray children's empty seats in our classes at school echoed full of terror, full of threat. A threat from something that comes out of the woods at night and takes children away, tearing at them with its long sharp and dirty claws til they were nothing.

I sat down, my legs brought up close to my body, resting under my chin. The Pastor's school gave us twenty minutes at midday to play out in the fields, and usually we would all be out, the grass full of stomping feet, some playing tig, some trying to climb a tree whilst one of the teacher's weren't looking; but since the disappearances fewer and fewer came out. And even I, only being nine at the time had noticed the odd child not showing up for class and Mrs Jansen discretely being given notes from parents. That day, during our twenty minute break I was minding my own business, trying not to look over at the treeline that lay only a field or two away, when I heard some of the other children talking.

One of them said, "And, so what was it?"

"Old Lady Peters said it looked like a woman, but not. In a long black cloak, its hood up, hanging over and casting a shadow so dark she never saw its face. Only the long straggly grey hair, the white hands…And she said…" A sullen looking boy said.

"What? What did she say?" A small girl asked desperately, who I recognised. Ana, one of the Neilsson children. My mother had worked with her mother in the fields over the harvest.

"She, she said it had long ragged nails on its hands, but too long to be nails, they looked more like claws."

A gasp rang out over the small crowd which had gathered round the boy and he looked up at me, eyes as wide as wells, and Ana looked back at me too, then past me, towards the trees. The afternoon was silent and over the bare skeletal branches of the forest, grey clouds loomed, shooting a gush of cold wind at all of us who were out on the field that day. The boy looked at me again, and what at first I thought was for dramatic effect I soon recognised as raw fear, left like an open wound on his face.

The next morning I was awoken early. The town's air filled with cries. I heard my mother's feet pound down the wooden stairs. I sat up in my bed and looked over to the crib where my baby sister lay fast asleep, breathing carelessly. The light outside had only just broken through the clouds that lined the horizon, and through the window I saw crowds of people rushing towards one house. The Neilsson's house. Through the din I made out one scream, sharp and full of pain. It was Elsa Neilsson. In her hands were the frayed and torn remains of the bedding she had found in her daughters room. Her fingers were bleeding, just as Rebecca Gray's were, and as she screamed and her husband held her tight, she threw away something that rolled over the wet and muddy floor; a doll.

In under a week the town had fallen into disarray. Children were being kept inside, first-borns especially. Mothers gripped onto their children's hands tight as they left for school, a look of excruciating fear in their eyes as they let go. It was as if the trees, the mist and the pine needles had turned the town mad. As I walked down a street dotted with our wooden houses I saw the faces of children plastered in the windows, longing to be out, but kept indoors for days. And then weeks passed and I hadn't seen three quarters of the children in our town outside. No shouting down the streets. No rabble in the backs of gardens. Just a terrifying and empty silence.

There were three families who weren't allowing their children to leave the house entirely, not even for school. First, the Triests, their mother was a sickly and suspicious woman who used to scare us children by telling us stories about bad spirits that exact revenge on those who hadn't been good. Second, were the Davidsons. Third, the Christoffs, our neighbours, living only one plot apart from our small house. Helena Christoff had a long and hard marriage with Gert, beginning with their troubles of having a baby and finishing with his tendency to gamble. Finally, last year they had a wonderful girl, named Marie. An angelic child, I would often look after her when not at school and when Helena Christoff and my own mother went off to work the fields.

The days propelled into darkness and the children of Marantown stewed. The faces at the windows became more and more drawn. Bigger and darker circles hanging under their eyes. One day, whilst out with my mother and sister, I looked up at the window of the Triest's large house and was sure their daughter was a ghost; so many bleak days passed, full of anxiety and terror of what may happen next.

The harrowing faces of the children at windows and locked in their rooms haunted me at night, and followed me into class from when I walked by them in the morning. The hideous, grey sky threatened overhead and once again, early one morning, I awoke to screams.

In one fell night the Davidsons' boys had been taken and not only that, but the dear, dear Helena Christoff, who had been such a good friend to our family, had her Marie, a girl of under two years, taken from her. The same recurring nightmare played out. The torn bedding, the pine needles, the mother's bloody hands, the empty bed and, the doll. Quickly people began to talk. My brother, who was fifteen at the time told me Old Lady Peters grabbed him whilst we were flooding out of church one day. She whispered, under her breath like it was a secret.

"The Drude," she mouthed, with wild eyes and pieces of dead leaf in her matted hair, "The Drude will come again. The people in this town are tainted boy. And they will pay."

Soon after the incident of the triple kidnapping the school closed. One early evening I sat on the lower branch of the young oak that stood at the back of my house, twiddling my plaits and the bits of ribbon that bound them, staring out to the trees. My mother had been next door for hours, trying to offer some comfort to poor Helena Christoff. As I daydreamed, the vast forest seemed to grow, its roots and branches crawling up towards the town, and in the distance I saw the pine trees. I looked on, in wonder and in terror for as I watched, the green pines turned white, and began falling to the floor and crawling towards me, ready to swallow me whole.

"Aline!" My mother shouted, and I almost jumped out of the tree in shock. I looked back to her, standing under the candle lamp that hung over our door. Then I looked once more to the forest. The pines were green again.

"Aline, come in! It will shortly be dark!" My mother beckoned, forcing a smile. She always tried to be brave, for me mostly. I rushed in as fast as I could, still fearful of the forest, of what gathered in there, in amongst the dead white pine needles, of The Drude.

It started at midnight. I awoke to the sound of distant rustling. Like all the trees in the land were moving slowly. I opened my eyes. The winter moon shone a pale and cold light through the thin cotton drapes at my window. Quite quickly the sound stopped and I fell back into a deep sleep. Startled into waking at two in the morning I heard a sound like the prying open of wooden panels, a dark creaking sound that filled my ears. My body seized up and I refrained from moving to the window to see what cruel thing made such a noise.

Somehow I managed to fall into an uneasy, shallow sleep.

Hours further into the morning I was awoken once more. This time though, there were no sounds that invaded my dreams, no creaking or rustling, only a feeling. A feeling as if something was in my room. I slowly opened my eyes, only a little, hoping to see the room lit up by moonlight with nothing there, but light escaped me. It seemed the entire room was painted in black, completely dark, and no light, not from the moon or sun, could penetrate. In the darkness I listened and laid completely still. Something broke through the staggering silence but refused to come forward, and I couldn't make it out. I listened on, harder and more concentrated, my heart thumping through my chest all the while.

Breathing.

It was breathing.

Just as I realised what the sound was, whatever was making it seemed to be conscious of the fact that I had noticed it, and a dreadful, stomach wrenching sound filled the room, a sound like metal being pried apart. I closed my eyes tight, wishing whatever the thing was away. Wishing for my father. Wishing to be saved. Wishing and hoping that I didn't end up like Jonathan Gray, or Ana, or little Marie.

Suddenly, the sound stopped. The room was quiet again. And I wondered if maybe it had all been some terrible nightmare. I lowered the cover from my eyes and, slowly opened them.

All at once a darkness so dense I thought I may be crushed engulfed me. And a screeching like that of a banshee filled my ears. I screamed, screamed loud and long and hard, until my throat felt like it might snap. Why was my brother not hearing me? Or my mother? Or neighbours? Tears ripped down my face and I stumbled about in a small dark space, not large enough to even stand up in. My heart felt as if it might break through my ribcage and in my head all I could see were the empty seats the Gray children left at school and how my seat would be empty. My mother would be left alone, Drew was never home and my sister, well she was barely two years old. I couldn't allow that. I fought and screamed but nothing seemed to help. Outside the darkness I heard something. A coarse ripping sound, like the world around me was being torn apart. *The bedsheets. It's ripping the bedsheets.* I heard the same jagged scraping and tearing as before. My heart beat even faster. Then, silence again. Only to be broken by a sound like the sprinkling of oats on the wooden floor. The pine needles.

Silence came again for a few short minutes and I was left blinking into the dark. Abruptly I was taken up from the floor, and the darkness swarmed all around me as I moved through the air at what felt like an enormous speed. The smell of soil, wet leaves and pine trees was all around me. Pungent and invasive. Still, I tumbled around in an unknown darkness that seemed to

# The Drude

surround me in eternity, until, I seemed to move downwards. In a flash of dark blue sky, stars and the moon, I fell from darkness, through the trees below me and was plunged into what felt like a pit of knives. My head hit something hard, and I was gone.

My eyes fluttered open, but something fell down on them preventing them from opening completely. I could smell the pines as if they were everywhere, but something else too, something coming from me, a metallic, bitter smell. Blood. I felt my arms with my hands and winced as my fingers ran over a hundred little pine needles that were stuck into my skin. My head was hazy and the temptation of sleep seemed to lure me in like a warm bath, telling me it was safe. But no. I knew I wouldn't wake up. I moved about. The pain was excruciating. But it kept me awake. I moved again, and again and again. I didn't know whether I was moving up or out or which way anything was, but I kept moving. For my mother, for my brother, for Helena Christoff who had lost her only child. Blood was running from my lips, my cheeks, my hands, my arms and I could feel my nightdress ripping. Then, my fingers broke out into the night. I felt grass. Wet, cool grass. My hands clung onto the ground and hauled my exhausted body from the torturous heap.

My breath blossomed up above my head and into the cold night as I lay there on my back, so ready to let sleep take me, but not willing to give up, not yet. I wiped the blood away from my eyes and picked out as many of the needles from my skin as I could, which only let out more blood. Standing up I stumbled back onto the trunk of a nearby tree. An oak. I couldn't have been too far from the town, but over the leafless branches of the oaks, back down into the darkness of the forest I saw the pines, dark and tall. I closed my eyes, breathing heavily, trying desperately to regain some of my strength. When I opened them they focused a little more on what I had managed to crawl out of. The thing in front of me was huge, it reached to the high branches of the trees it surrounded. An immense stack of pine needles, all white, all dead, and yet, they seemed to be moving. As my breath slowed and my heart calmed my eyes moved over the smaller details, and then I saw it. Sticking out at the bottom, not five feet from me, lifeless and limp, was a small hand. A child's hand. In the dark behind the oak trees I heard that same scratching and wailing like some great structure being ruptured. A wave of fear and dread coursed through my body and before

I knew what my feet were doing I was running. I didn't care for the blood, nor the pain. I just ran. And ran. I saw nothing around me, only looked to the stars above, shining like white fireflies in the sky. Tears fled from my eyes and fell behind me as I flew over the forest floor. My legs ached and nearly gave way as I ran, unyielding, over the rough turf. The pain was unbearable and just as I was about to give in, I saw the steeple of our town's church. White and proud against the night sky. Then I saw the houses. Then the trees started to part. How long had I been running? I didn't know, nor did I care. I broke into the open field and away from the trees, almost falling on the slippery wet grass. I saw my house. Small and welcoming. My tears mixed with my blood as I rounded the corner of the house opposite mine and I almost began screaming with joy when I spotted a small hooded figure moving towards my door. I stopped instantly, scraping my arm against the corner of the house I was next to. My breath was heavy and loud, but the figure didn't seem to hear me. It entered my house, silently pushing away the wooden trunk that was behind the door.

My eyes gleamed under the light of the moon and a shiver ran over me.

The path up to my house was imprinted with small wet and muddy shoe prints. The door creaked slightly as my hand grabbed it for some balance. I couldn't hear anything. The house was as quiet as it always was. I moved up the stairs, careful not to press too much on the fourth step up as it always made a loud, pitiful squeak as you went up. The muddy shoe prints lead up away from the staircase, over the hall and…and…to my room. Once again that night I felt as though I may be sick from the fear that burned in my stomach, but I swallowed it and kept moving on.

Through my open door I could smell that same musty scent, old leaves, the forest. I dreaded what I might see. As I came round to the opening, I saw a black silhouetted figure, hunched over my bed, whispering madly, and shaking.

I took another step forward.

Being careful to not make any sound.

*Creak.* My toes fell on the uneven floorboard at the entrance to my room. The hooded figure turned, hands shaking. Lips chattering like they were repeating some wicked chant. And as it turned its face, the light coming in through my window, the last moonlight of the morning, shone on its face. *Her* face. My jaw dropped, all the blood in my body fell to the floor as I saw her face, her features and matched them up with Marantown's Old Lady Peters. And she smiled at me, revealing yellow and crooked teeth, and a cruel devilish glint in her eye. And in her hand there was a doll.

A doll that looked just like me.

"The Drude," she had said.

"The Drude will come again. The people in this town are tainted, boy. And they will pay."

~o~

For my short story *The Drude* everything started with me thinking about *The Uncanny* in my prose class at university. We did a week on uncanny short fiction, and I was enamoured with Edgar Allen Poe's tales. I had also been learning about it in another module at university on the Gothic. The idea of something indescribable has also always interested me. Fear is a big part of everything I write, whether it's fear of exposing aspects of yourself, anxiety, horror at something uncanny or even fear of more vast and complex ideas that encapsulate our lives, like freedom or love.

This piece focuses on how fearing something can in itself be destructive. Environments in my tale that should be safe become dangerous, such as the houses that the children are being kept in by their parents, where they slowly become more and more ill. This effect of the familiar becoming unfamiliar and unsafe is an important aspect of *The Uncanny* that I wanted to include in my short story. The monster, the thing, 'The Drude' itself isn't really too important, what it is exactly doesn't need to be made clear. It is the result of it's presence, the closeness of the forest, the disappearing children that I hope gives the story it's real effect.

For a long time poetry felt the most natural for me, being able to say something important or personal always felt normal through the poetic form. It has only been through finding writers, whether they be novelists like Patrick Ness and Philip Pullman or short fiction writers, whom I love so dearly and from learning so much about writing at York St John University that I have come to realise that my poetry can be in my prose. And it so often is.

# CHRISTIAN ROBSHAW
## THE END IS THE MIDDLE

Christian Robshaw is a young writer and journalist currently living in North London. He read English with Creative Writing at the University of Aberdeen, and now wastes his intellect writing reviews of mostly cheap horror films at mrrumsey.com, and 1000-ish-word analyses of cultural minutiae at mediocrebatman.wordpress.com. Earlier this year he completed his first novel, *Wankers*, for which he is currently seeking representation.

With a shiver the house began to collapse in on itself. I tried to make a wry comment to Jill about the obvious symbolism of the structure in which we had existed crashing down around us, but I couldn't make myself heard over the noise. When I saw her expression, I didn't bother trying to repeat myself. I don't think it would have helped her at all. She looked at me with horror, as if she'd come to a realisation I hadn't. Sighing, I began our slow walk toward the end of the beach, where a new dawn was already rising for us. We would walk into that dawn, and into the final part of our lives together, but Jill resisted; she pleaded with me.

"Please, don't you understand? This is *it*! This is it and I don't want to *go*."

"There's nothing to fear in it, Jill, we're young yet and we have stories left." The long grass swayed gently in a breeze I couldn't feel. The breakers broke indifferently.

"No, you're wrong, it's over, there's nothing beyond that sunset."

I looked out at it, a hand shielding my eyes. I saw narrative possibility.

"Listen," she spoke to me in the tone a lawyer might use with a client, "you must understand. This is the end of the story. There isn't anything beyond that sunset." Here her lawyer's tone began to choke with tearful desperation. "I don't want to go, don't make me go, I want to live, I don't want our story to end."

"Nonsense!" I told her, skimming down the page. "Look, we're barely at the middle yet. There's plenty left in us. You see that asterisk? That marks roughly the middle of the story, see, and it continues. You'll know it's ending when we get to 'A long groan rang out and'…and what?" The final part I said mostly to myself, but Jill simpered a little on hearing it, with the kind of sympathy one might have for a dog about to be put down. What was she driving at?

It looks like a strange ending, I'll admit, but I know I'll understand it when I reach it. One can trust a story to play out; no matter what narrative oddities come into it, an ending is an ending. It's true, they're sad to reach, but they all strike the same note of emotional fulfilment, the right kind of exquisite aching. It wouldn't do to end with pleading and with desolation, or with nastiness, or subversive tricks.

"Please," she tried again, her voice cracking. "Remember this story's title, don't do this to us."

"Jill," I told her resolutely. "A title is a title, a story is a story; we have our rôles to play and this simply won't do."

Taking Jill's arm in mine, I led her slowly down the beach. Tears poured from her eyes, soaking her jacket, but my head was high as I walked from the remains of the beach house that had held us. An aeroplane's vapour trail slowly relaxed, dispersed through the sky by another unknown breeze. A lone seagull in a dune pecked at a hidden treasure in an abandoned can, and Jill and I walked on into the rising sun, she still bewailing a perceived doom I couldn't understand.

I awoke with my head in my hands, a small pool of saliva gently sticking my open mouth to my sleeve. I was thirsty and Jill was nowhere to be seen. I made ice tea from a powder, pressing the glass against the ice dispenser on the

## The End Is The Middle

fridge, then wandered the beach house. I knew the house. At times it gave me the comforting feeling I might have built it with my own hands – which step creaked, which pipe under which floorboard settled itself at night, exactly what pitch it groaned at during a high wind. I could gather the o'clock by the pattern the rays of the sun cast across the floorboards.

From the window of the bedroom I could see almost the whole beach, lit now with the weird purple glow of the pre-dawn. Already I could feel time distending, the air awash with the pretty finality of an ending. It wasn't that I was glad to be going, but I enjoyed the sense of appropriateness, of having fulfilled my duty. I was stoic, like the soldier returning home.

I finished my ice tea with a slight slurp like a vacuum unsealing. Two large blocks of freshly threshed ice pressed against my teeth, sending a shiver through me. I still didn't know where Jill was, but the matter didn't seem pressing. When one is in the grip of any terrible emotion, it's worth taking a few minutes to simply experience it, to feel it crushing everything inside, fighting to burst its way out.

As I said, a pleasurable sense of propriety prevented everything else from overwhelming me. I showered just longer than was necessary, basking in the onomatopoeia that crashed around me, before dressing – a black suit with a no less black shirt, open-collared, conveying dignity without a stifling surfeit of formality – and brushing my teeth.

I made sure to clear my mind, making a point of simply experiencing to the full the dull, familiar taste of mint, the sensation of paste becoming froth, the repetitive scour of bristle on coated molars. All of this was circling the edge of my clear mind when a sound from the attic roused me.

Jill was there, stacks of her girlhood comics around her, a sledgehammer in hand and a crowbar at her feet. "I tried-" she began to explain, "We need a beginning, Jack. Who are we? What came before this?"

"What do you mean, before?"

"This is the beach house, isn't it? This is where our lives as we know them have taken place, but what were we before? Where does our story begin?"

"I understand coming to the attic, Jill, insofar as your childish things have been put away up here, but," I smiled, without meaning to, at her cute folly, "if you want the foundations of our story, shouldn't you be looking in the basement?"

I regretted having said it. A manic look flashed across her face and she flew down the stairs, two or three at a time. I followed as closely after as I could manage.

When I reached her in the basement, she was crowbarring up slabs of the paving as quickly as she could manage, sweating with the determination of an idée fixe. I found her wish for a beginning sweet in its own way, but foolish. My only real concern was that it might give her difficulty when our ending came, but I was sure things would turn out alright.

Jill fell to her knees, digging with her hands into the foundations of the structure. She unearthed notes, idle doodles, stray thoughts and unused dialogue. The more she dug into the foundations, the weaker the narrative structure became. Jill, apparently, had discovered some oddity of construction which she tried to explain to me, but, as the dust of our lives began to fall from the ceiling, the pillars creaking, I realised the house was collapsing. A fine ending, I took it for, if an obvious one. I tugged at Jill's sleeve, but she kept talking away, excitedly.

Perturbed, I tried to explain to her that our story was at its end. She was talking about endings, too, but not in a way that made any sense to me.

"Come *on*, girl", I told her. "Don't you have anything to say? Some tragic-ironic summation of events? This is *it*! This is how we'll be remembered." Sighing, my hopes of an exquisitely aching ending dashed, I grabbed her sleeve, dragging her from our doomed abode. A long groan rang out and

~o~

Famously, the one question writers are sick of being asked is, "Where do you get your ideas from?". The question as it stands fails to account for the mysterious workings of creativity, as if we could all be Conrad or Hemingway had we only had the same experiences. Well, in this case at least, I can point to a very precise source of inspiration: toilet graffiti.

Specifically, it was a piece of toilet graffiti which read, "In the end, everything will be OK. If it's not OK, it's not the end." *How trite*, I thought to myself as I reached for the toilet roll, *what rot*. Actually, I'd always been fascinated by endings – haunted by last lines of books or final episodes of television programmes – but for reasons much more complex and bittersweet. The equation of ending with glib, neat, wrapped-up-ness irritated me in a way I couldn't explain, any more than I could explain why I was so keen on endings. In any case I was determined to really stick it to that anonymous graffitist with a story skewering his naïveté. He became Jack, so blindly, breezily determined that things must work out that he walks unknowingly to his own literary doom. From there, the rest of the story fell into place naturally enough, with a few details – the beach, the angry seagull – supplied by my Aberdeen surroundings at the time, and an offhand mention of powdered ice tea simply because, having just discovered the stuff, it was on my mind.

# HANNAH M KING
## THE DORSTAN FALL

Hannah King is a twenty-two-year-old writer, who is from Suffolk, England. She is currently reading Creative and Professional Writing at Canterbury Christ Church University. At present, she is working on her long term project *The Dorston Legacy* a Fantasy trilogy that follows the adventures and struggles of a medieval Princess. She also enjoys spending time with friends and family, as well as quiet nights in with a good book or film.

"Up high," her father called out, slashing at her head. The sword clanged, as Katelyn parried. "Left," he instructed. His blade came whistling towards her. She moved on instinct, meeting it. The reassuring clack made her father click his teeth together. He paused, smiling down at her.

"Very good," he said. She smiled, and nodded her thanks. "And break."

Her father retreated a few steps; wiping the sweat from his brow. Katelyn turned, spinning her sword in a practiced motion, waiting in earnest. The look of admiration she received from her father did not go unnoticed. Mere weeks into her training and already, she felt stronger, more sure of herself, her body and her ability. She'd suffered a few cuts and bruises but, as she told herself again and again, it was all part of the learning process. A process that was changing her into someone better - a warrior.

"Shall we pick up the pace?" He asked, a mischievous twinkle in his eye.

She spun her sword once more. "Whatever suits you, Father," she teased, smiling innocently at him.

He laughed, turning sideways; positioning his feet shoulder-width apart, and angling his front foot. He extended his longsword, and the early morning light danced on the edge. Katelyn imitated his stance. She took a deep breath.

"I will not be giving any direction," he warned, with a cunning smirk. "Whatever happens now, it is your own."

He leaped forward without warning. Katelyn swung, intercepting his attack. The resounding clang echoed through the hall, sending a pleasant shiver down her spine. Her father moved swiftly into a counter-parry of his own. He dropped into a crouch, and hacked at her ankles. She jumped over the blade. He vaulted onto his feet; launching into a series of quick, short blows.

Katelyn blocked every swing.

She felt the stirrings of excitement in her gut. She always did, when sparring with her father. Her other tutors were continuously gentle with her, treating her like some fragile flower about to bruise. They were slow in their delivery of techniques and criticism. Her father was not. He was insistent, and demanding but ever so encouraging. No one exposed her potential like he did. Katelyn trusted his judgement, his harsh but real critique; for it was the only way to do better, to be better.

Their swords continued to block and stab, the conversation of their weapons echoing through the great hall. Her father parried with a grunt. He slashed at her torso, connecting with air as Katelyn spun quickly out of the way. She lashed out, swiping at his shoulder. He blocked, quickly, parried again, and then swung. The reach of his sword was too long. She leaned back, watching the point pass over her.

Safe.

Quickly finding her feet, she struck out. Clank. Metal on metal. It was then a game of strengths. She pushed. Her arms locked and shook. He shoved; biting his lip against the unexpected struggle. Katelyn could feel her father's hoarse, warm breath rubbing against her cheek. She could feel her own heart hammering against her rib cage; consumed by adrenaline, running on heat and exhilaration.

She narrowed the distance between them; sliding her sword along her father's. Up close, like this, it was Katelyn's petite blade that held the advantage.

"Is someone growing weary?" she taunted with a wicked grin. Sparring with words was almost as much fun as sparring with swords, and she'd had little opportunity to practice. Her teachers were always so serious. They never appreciated her humour.

"Never," he sneered, his face turning red.

He blew in her face and jumped back. The blades shrilled and sang apart. He attacked without pause; hitting the outer rim of her sword. Katelyn blocked his advance, barely. A bead of sweat rolled into her eye. She blinked through the sting. Her father swung again and again, battering her sword. On a drawback, she faked to the right, and then lunged to the left; aiming, hoping, to nick his side. One drop of blood would assure her victory. But her intention was quickly thwarted. Her father's triumphant laugh ricocheted through the hall.

"Almost, but not quite," he bellowed. His tone and smile were kind, but mocking all the same. Katelyn snorted and glared; her jaw taking on a stubborn set.

"Then let me try again," she said.

Katelyn pushed him away with a strength and determination she had never felt before. She beat at her father's sword, hard, and followed it up with immediate and fierce remise. But yet again, his sword was there to meet every attack.

They moved about the room, their boots squeaking along the polished floor. The sound of their blades called into the air. Her father swung his sword in a wild, diagonal cut; a powerful but slack blow that left him completely exposed. His blade trilled through the air, running towards her. Katelyn dodged out of the way, the momentum of his swing carrying her well within his range. He shifted his feet, trying to regain his balance, his advantage, but not before she struck him across the forearm. More than fabric was torn. Red dribbled quickly from the long, shallow gash.

He faltered, and his longsword clattered to the floor. Victory. The glorious sound tolled through the sudden silence of the room.

"Yield," demanded Katelyn, whipping the sword point over her father's heart. He raised his hands and laughed; the warm sound vibrating from within.

"I yield. I yield," he said, as she lowered her sword. A cute sound escaped her lips. "By the gods, Katelyn. Well done. Very, very well done."

"Thank you," she said, red in her cheeks. She slid the castillon blade into the scabbard at her hip. "You fought well yourself."

He chortled, bending down to retrieve his sword. "I've taught you too well, my girl. You are a true match," he commended.

"But?" She dragged out the syllable. Katelyn crossed her arms, her head tilted to the side expectantly.

He smirked, pointing his sword to the ground. "Your footwork," he revealed.

"Again?" she exclaimed. "I've been working hard, I swear. Sir Michael has been putting me through my paces-"

"Learning and doing are two very different things, Katelyn."

"I know," she sighed, releasing her dark hair from its band. Falling, it surpassed her shoulders, and tickled the back of her neck.

"And Master Turner is trained. You are not."

She gasped. "Are you insulting my ability? Haven't you hurt me enough today?" she played, holding a hand over her heart.

"I wouldn't dare," he laughed, cupping her warm cheek. "I only mean to give you good council, my dearest."

"I know, Father," she huffed, staring in to his smiling, silver eyes; eyes she had inherited proudly. "And I am always grateful for it."

He bent down and kissed her forehead. His slight beard tickled her skin. Katelyn closed her eyes and smiled; enjoying this rare show of affection.

"No man became a master overnight, Kat," he said. "A disciplined mind and good instruction will take you far. Remember that, and time will do the rest."

Katelyn nodded, hope and refound fortitude forming within. Her father always had a way with words.

"How's your arm?" she asked, watching the white of his tunic stain red. He glanced down and shrugged.

"Nothing yarrow can't fix," he beamed.

The great timber doors of the hall flew open, suddenly, roaring like thunder. They both started, then peered round.

A knight of her father's guard rushed in through the arch of the door. He was in full armour, enamelled steel from neck to heel. A long, navy cloak hugged his shoulders and fluttered behind him. Morning light danced in his yellow locks and green eyes. A longsword bounced on his hip. His right hand was balanced on the diamond shaped pommel of the hilt. His direct, stiff pace was troubling, but no more so than his expression.

"Nicholas?" Her father called.

"Pardon the incursion my Lord, but we've received word from Baldon," Nicholas gasped, reaching into his cloak.

"From Maxim?" her father frowned, stepping towards him. "Why? What's happened?"

"As many as five thousand men are marching on the city," the knight reported. Regret clouded his features. From his cloak, he revealed a long piece of parchment; rolled up tightly; its crimson seal unbroken.

"What?" The King snatched the parchment. He tore at the seal and read quickly; his brows snapped together. Katelyn gnawed on her bottom lip, and wrapped her arms tightly around her waist; terror and worry swelling in her gut.

"Who are they? Who commands them?" Her father barked, angrily.

"They call themselves the Justice, my Lord," Nicholas replied quickly, almost trembling. "They wear black armour, and bear a skull insignia."

"Who do they follow? Who is it, Nicholas?"

Nicholas pulled in a breath. "They are being led by Drake Lore, Your Majesty."

Katelyn frowned, the name unfamiliar to her, and glanced nervously at her father. A vehemence overtook him. His lip curled, his cheeks burned scarlet, and his knuckles whitened around the parchment; savaging the edges.

"Will I ever be rid of that accursed man?" he murmured. His breath quickened; released in hard puffs.

Nicholas took a small step back, looking to the floor. Katelyn could not blame him. Her father was known best for his temper and fierce stubbornness, but he was also loved for his kindness, fair judgement and incredible strength. Merits he needed reminding of every once in a while.

"Father?" she whispered, placing a soft hand on his arm. He flinched under her touch, but she stood her ground. She watched him, patiently, and waited for the storm in his heart and mind to pass.

After a long, tense moment, he sighed and placed a gentle hand on top of hers. A tender caress, and Katelyn knew he was well within his right mind again.

"Nicholas, send immediate word to my council. I need them in the war room as soon as possible," he ordered. "And spread word to the rest of the guard. I need their commitment and service."

The knight nodded. "Yes, my Lord."

"Send the messengers to the lower town and outer villages. We need men of good, strong age. Tell the blacksmiths to fire up the furnaces. We need weapons. As much as they can muster. Ready the horses. I will ride out as soon as I am able."

Katelyn turned her head away; a sudden and indescribable pressure forming behind her eyes. The pain prickled her mind, and her world blurred into a dull mass of colour. *No,* a desperate voice whispered. She couldn't appear weak. She couldn't cry, though her heart was breaking. She couldn't appear weak. Not in front of her father. Not in front of Nicholas. One breath, and every tension, every emotion rolled back into the shadows.

"And return word to Baldon," her father continued. "The House of Ivone will not stand alone in this fight."

"Very good, your Majesty. My Lady." Nicholas bowed, and walked quickly from the hall. His sword clinked against his tasset made of chainmail.

Katelyn watched him go, feeling a strange sympathy for him. As long as she had known him, he'd always been a jovial, high spirited fellow. He entertained, and demanded the attention, respect and fidelity of his audience. But now, in the shadow of war, a hardness and presence had overtaken him. She could not imagine how difficult it was to deliver such grave news.

Her father sighed heavily. "I am to go to war."

Katelyn turned her face into his shoulder. Her lip trembled. She said nothing. Nothing she said now would soothe the regret and pain of what was to come. Her father would leave for Baldon, and he would fight the Justice. He would return home, or die on the battlefield. She whimpered, and her father pressed his lips to her crown; shushing and bringing her closer.

"I do not choose this path lightly, my dearest," he murmured, rubbing circles into the skin of her hand. "I hate war. I hate the cost, and the whole uncertainty." He turned abruptly, and hooked her chin with his index finger. His silver eyes bored into hers. "But Maxim is our ally, my friend since boyhood, and your godfather. I cannot desert him. You understand?"

"I understand, Father," she told him.

Truly, she did understand, but she despised it all the same. Belran had seen eight years of peace. Not a single word or whisper of rebellion or repression. The people were content with their lives, and their ruling family. But now, like moths to a flame, they were being drawn into a battle not of their choosing. Their husbands, brothers and sons would be called to serve and protect the realm from the brutality of the mercenaries, who sought to claim everything they held dear. Was it right to ask such a sacrifice? No. Was it necessary? Unfortunately so.

"Good girl," he murmured, kissing her head again. "Now, I must find and inform your mother of the news. Would you like some dinner brought to you? You've worked hard this morning."

She shook her head. "I think I'll practice for a while longer," she said quietly.

"Very well," her father sighed. He turned on his heel and made his way to the door. Katelyn was drawing her sword, when he suddenly shouted. "Find your feet!"

She allowed herself a small laugh. "Bind your wound!"

Her father disappeared down the corridor, but she could still hear the echo of his great laughter. She closed her eyes; trapping the sound, the memory of this day, in her mind for all time. In a matter of days, hours even, her father would depart and she, her mother and their people would be left to a fate unknown. She would no longer hear her father's voice, nor feel his warm embrace. She would no longer experience the thrill of sparring with him, sharing repartee or wisdom. And she would lose him to the blood and glory of war. She trembled, looking to the ceiling. A thousand, bright faced Saints stared down at her; waiting on her word.

"Curse the Justice," whispered Princess Katelyn, her prayer sailed through the space, a mere gasp in the silence. "Curse them. Bring them Hell. Bring my father home."

~o~

As a novel, *The Dorston Fall* was developed from an old idea. It was still of the Fantasy genre and of a similar structure and plot, but it lacked foundation and efficient planning. With this in mind, I put it aside and concentrated on other pieces, as well as academic work. It was in 2013, when I returned to the idea and set about making something amazing. I spent weeks researching and arranging events and conflicts, producing character profiles and back stories. In short, creating a whole new world in which to set the story.

The Fantasy genre has always held a special place in my heart. Purely, because there is so much you can do with it. You can create new worlds, creatures and foes. You can bring magic and myth back to life: dragons, unicorns, fairies, witches and wizards, anything your imagination can conjure. Having grown up with the likes of Disney, and work by J.K Rowling, Rick Riordan, Liz Kessler and Maggie Stiefvater, the idea of magic, adventure and romance has always appealed, and will continue to do so for many years to come.

Growing up, stories helped me to escape the worries and stresses of everyday life, and I long to do the same for others. I want to empower the downtrodden, and give hope and comfort to those who need it most. And, as any writer, I long to see my novels on the shelves of bookshops and to live happily, knowing I am inspiring someone.

# MEGAN ATKINS
## TEMPORAL TRACERS

Megan Atkins is an eighteen-year-old writer from Northamptonshire. She is currently reading Psychology, English Language and Literature and Health and Social Care at the local secondary school. A poem by her has been published in the past. In her spare time she enjoys volunteering with a local Pre-school and walking the dog.

### 20th December 2016

Get up. Go to work. Come home. Watch TV with my flatmate. That was my plan. Just an ordinary day. But sometimes the most extraordinary days begin like the most ordinary.

You would expect that living in a small English town would be boring. And most days you'd be right on the mark.

But sometimes, on rare occasions, the impossible can happen.

I expect now would be a good time to introduce myself. My name is Jessica Barrett. I'm five foot five and I live in Spencer Gardens with my best mate Jodie. Lived. I meant I lived in Spencer Gardens with Jodie. It was our home for two years. From leaving school at eighteen until my death at age twenty.

You never really know what's going to happen. You make plans, talk about the future but all you can do is hope and pray that you'll get to see it unfold. If you do then you're one of the lucky ones.

In a way I suppose I was lucky. After all, things could have turned out much worse.

It was a snowy morning. Ice made the roads and paths treacherous. Most people wouldn't go out on a morning like that, preferring to stay home rather than brave the cold and go to work.

Personally I'm not a fan of the snow. Scandalous, I know. As a kid, it's exciting. Schools close and you get to stay home and play outside with your friends all day before going in to a toasty warm house. As a teenager I found it to be a brilliant excuse to stay inside with a hot drink and a *Supernatural* box-set. But as an adult, it's an all-round nightmare.

I pulled my sock monkey hat down further by the braids as I walked through the alley next to the frame shop. (So shoot me, I took a short cut.) As I crossed the road I blew into my hands, trying to get some feeling other than pain into my fingers. As I walked I reminded myself to get my gloves back from Jodie when I got home.

I ducked through another alley in order to get to the high street.

The high street. That was my downfall. I'd checked so carefully. There hadn't been anything coming either way, I was sure of it. I even walked the extra few feet to use the crossing at the traffic lights. I waited patiently for the light and once it went green started to cross.

The car came out of nowhere. Then…

Bang!

The last thing I saw was the concerned blue eyes of the driver before I fell out of consciousness.

## 20th December 2216

I awoke in an impossibly white room. The bed beneath me was as soft as a cloud; the light a dim yellow. I began to notice cupboards and drawers that hadn't been visible at first glance. Wondering if I was in heaven I barely noticed when a doctor walked in. Not heaven then, I decided; if it were the doctors would be younger and much more attractive. No, scratch that. There wouldn't be any doctors at all. I don't suppose I thought that through.

As it stood, this doctor was… podgy would be the polite way of putting it. His hair was at the point of being practically non-existent and what little was left had turned a dull grey. Black piggy eyes studied me closely as he picked up what appeared to be my charts.

"Pleased to see you've finally woken up." His voice was as dull as his appearance.

"How long was I out?" I asked, propping myself up on my elbows to get a better look at him. I was surprised to discover I wasn't in any pain. Surely I should be after being hit by a car.

"Either a few hours or a couple of hundred years. Depends on your perspective."

"Right... wait... WHAT!?" A couple of hundred years. Those words hit me harder than the car. "What do you mean a couple of hundred years!?"

"I'm really not the person to tell you."

"Then why did you mention it?" I snapped. I've never liked having information withheld and this seemed even more important than anything else that had ever been kept from me.

"I wasn't thinking."

"Clearly."

"Is there anything I can get for you?"

"Yes. Someone to explain what the hell is going on."

He paused for a moment before nodding and leaving the room.

I must have nodded off again, because the next thing I heard was a man speaking. His voice was rich like melted chocolate and honey, his tone soothing. I just lay for a moment, listening to the sound of his voice, demands all but forgotten as I let the sound wash over me.

"Miss Barrett." I rubbed my eyes and sat up, before focusing on the newcomer.

He looked to be in his seventies. His hair was white as freshly fallen snow and looked slightly windswept. But it was his eyes that really caught my attention. Oceanic blue and oddly fam... "You hit me with a car!"

He had the good grace to look a little guilty. "Sorry about that. But it was necessary."

"How was trying to kill me necessary!?"

"So we could recruit you," he said, as if it should have been obvious.

"What do you mean recruit me? Recruit me for what?" I had to force myself to calm down. Losing my temper would not have got me anywhere.

"Jessica Barrett." The way he said my name made it sound as if it had been given some kind of undeserved grandeur. "How would you like to be a Time Traveller?"

"You have got to be kidding me."

"I'm not."

"There's no such thing as time travel."

"Yes there is." That didn't make any sense. If Time Travel was really possible surely people (other than nuts conspiracy theorists) would know.

"No there isn't. We'd know about it" I said.

"No you wouldn't."

"Why not?"

"Because you've all been made to believe that Time Travel is a work of fiction."

"Why?"

"Because if people of your time knew, it could change the course of our current time line." Kind of like in 'A Sound of Thunder', I thought to myself. Change one small detail, kill one butterfly, and the whole course of human history is altered.

"Where am I?"

"Temporal Tracers' Headquarters. You're in the medical wing."

Feeling absolutely none the wiser, I had to ask. "Temporal Tracers?"

"We work as a kind of police force. Since the invention of time travel, terrorists have realised that if they don't like the way something works, they can go back and change it. It is our job to stop that from happening."

"What's this got to do with me?" I asked, fully expecting to regret it.

"You've been recruited."

"Recruited?" I blinked at him still completely clueless.

"We recruit the best and brightest from throughout history and you've been chosen to join us." I raised an eyebrow at that.

"How am I the best or brightest? The only reason that could be the case is if I were the only person in existence. Ever."

"You're underestimating yourself-"

"No I'm not." I interrupted. I mean seriously. Me? Best or brightest? I really don't think so. Someone must have made a mistake somewhere.

"Your knowledge of history will prove most useful to us." He finished as if I'd never even been speaking.

"Who the hell are you to try and judge me anyway? What gives you the right to just snatch me away from all my family and friends? Press ganging me into joining your group of time travelling coppers." Frustration was beginning to bubble over. I didn't want to be here and I didn't ask to be here. All I wanted was to go to work for a few hours and hopefully try to make a little more than minimum wage.

"My name is Henry Duke. I'm the head of this department. If I hadn't recruited you, another car would have come down that road. The driver would have been driving at 50 miles per hour and been unable to stop when they hit a patch of ice and you would have been killed."

I was lost for words. I was supposed to be dead? At 20, you always believe yourself to be indestructible. You think nothing could happen to you. Now all of a sudden I'm meant to be dead and there's nothing I could have done to stop it.

"It's your choice. Either you join us or, I'm afraid, you die." His voice was gentle, understanding. "You don't have to decide now, but we need to know when you've made your choice."

"How do I know you're not screwing with me?" I asked, after all this was too ridiculous for any kind of serious contemplation, yet somehow I was inclined to believe him. I couldn't place exactly what it was but something made me want to trust him.

"You don't know. Not for certain. The only way you can know is accepting or declining my offer."

"Ok. I'll do it." It was a no brainer really. Get to see any point in history, or be sent to my death. What would you choose?

"In which case, if you want to get dressed, you can attend an introduction." Without waiting for an answer he left me to change.

I pondered my decision as I put on the clothes I had been left. On the one hand I didn't fancy the idea of dying anytime in the near future. On the other hand, however, I resented being given no choice in the matter even more.

I checked my appearance in the mirror. A pair of tired green eyes stared back at me. My brown curls had gone flat on one side from where I had been sleeping and I used my hand to fluff them up slightly.

It was only then that I noticed the clothes. They weren't what I was wearing when I was hit by the car. Where I had been wearing skinny jeans and a Christmas jumper, I now wore a short black skirt and a well-fitting white blouse.

"Ok." I whispered softly to my reflection. "You'll be ok."

With those words of comfort still echoing in my head I stepped out of the room.

Whilst I hadn't really expected Duke to have hung around I also hadn't expected a handsome young man to be waiting in his place.

"Who're you?" I asked, watching with something akin to awe as silver eyes met mine.

"My name is Maxwell Keen." He explained. His accent was upper class, English and sounded like an officer pulled straight from a film about WWI.

"I'm Jess Barrett." I told him, offering my hand. As I looked him over, taking in his strong yet slender physique and soft brown locks of hair that seemed to be falling over his eyes every few seconds despite his repeated attempts to brush them away. I decided I wouldn't mind getting to know him.

"You know," he muttered to himself, completely ignoring my offered hand, "I will never understand why girls need to show so much skin. Even the whores in my day didn't show so much."

Then again, maybe I would mind. I thought irritably as I lowered my hand. "Did you just call me a slut?"

"A what?" He looked slightly startled, as if he hadn't thought I'd be able to hear him.

"A whore as you so delicately put it."

"Oh. Well you must admit it's a tad too much, isn't it."

"I'll have you know this is the height of fashion where and when I come from."

"That says a lot really doesn't it."

"Just because you might be from the Dark Ages doesn't mean the rest of us have to play by your rules. I bet if you had your way women wouldn't be able to work or have the vote."

"Oh no. You're another of those bloody suffragettes aren't you?"

"No I am not." I'd finally snapped. "I don't need to be because we got rid of people like you a long time ago."

I didn't know where I was going, I just knew I had to leave. I didn't want to be around this sexist idiot any longer.

As I attempted to find my bearings somehow I bumped into a girl. She was taller than me and had dark hair and blue eyes. "Hey, are you OK?" She asked, a look of concern on her face.

"Yeah, I'm OK. Sorry about that. I'm a little lost."

"Oh." She thought for a moment then realisation lit up her face. "Oh, you're a new recruit."

"Yeah, I was supposed to attend an introduction."

"I can help you with that, follow me." She started walking down a corridor in the other direction to the way I had come. "So how did you manage to get lost? What happened to your guide?" She asked as we walked through what appeared to be an office area. There were hundreds of cubicles each filled with a desk and someone working. The variety of technology within the one room was almost overwhelming. There was everything ranging from paper and pencil to holographic computers being used.

"There was a guy waiting outside my room but he said something stupid, I got annoyed and left." I explained.

"Who was it?" Emily asked after a moment's thought.

"I think he said his name was Maxwell Keen."

"Yeah, Max can be difficult at times," she explained as she took me to wherever I was meant to be. Difficult. That was an understatement. "He's a sweetie really, he's just struggling to adapt to the changes."

"How long has he been here then?" I asked, curiosity quickly escalating.

"About six months. But he died in 1916 so it's a bit of a change from what he's used to."

"Yeah, I suppose it would be."

"Though I'll admit, one thing you said was a little strange."

"What's that?"

"Duke doesn't usually deal with new agents himself. He gets a current agent to do it for him. So why did he deal with you personally? I mean to be honest, most days you'd struggle to get him to leave his office."

I shrugged casually. "Dunno. Maybe he just got bored of hanging around in his office all day."

"Yeah… maybe…"

"So what's first?" I asked, somewhat eager to change the topic.

"I'm running a quick introduction then you're starting training. It'll likely be a little different than when you're from but you'll get used to it."

"So… when are you from?" I asked, tilting my head to the side slightly as I looked up at her.

"2015."

"How did you die?" I asked, curiosity increasing.

She paused for a moment, glancing at me, trying to decide if she should say anything. Eventually she caved. "There was a terrorist attack, in the building where I worked."

"Is that the one in London? A government building was blown up and six killed?"

"Yeah. All of whom were recruited. Can't say Curtis would be best pleased."

"Curtis?"

"Our old boss. Long story."

"I've got plenty of time you know."

"You don't actually and even if you did it's classified. Sorry. Anyway this is where I'll have to leave you I'm afraid. I need to grab a few things before the talk." We were stood in a long corridor with doors either side of the passageway and seeming to stretch for miles. Ok, maybe that was a bit of an exaggeration but you get my point. "You want the door at the very end." She clarified for my benefit.

I nodded, mentally repeating the instruction to make sure I got it. "Door at the end. Ok. Thanks."

"See ya in a minute, Jess."

"Yeah, See ya Emily." But she was gone before I'd even finished speaking.

The room was, for want of a better description, an old fashioned lecture theatre. No, forget old. Ancient is a better word. It even had a blackboard! Despite the lecture theatre's rather large size there were only about 10 people sat in there. I located a seat towards the front just as Emily came bustling in with a pile of papers in her arms.

"Good morning everyone." She greeted with a smile as she placed her papers on the desk at the front. "My name's Emily Murphy and I'm here to introduce you to the wonderful world of the temporal tracers."

She told us about the organisation we had been recruited to and about how it had been created in 2200 in order to prevent disruptions in the current timeline (mostly stuff Duke had told me in the hospital room).

She then went on to talk for the next hour or so about the various training exercises we would be going through for the next few months. From survival training to foreign languages. Weapons to time travel.

"The only thing left to do is warn you. This is a dangerous job and not everyone survives. Some don't even make it through training so stay safe and good luck. I hope we'll see you all at the end of training."

## **17th April 2217**

Training was hell. That's the only way of putting it. The only relief was no-one died. Two people dropped out, deciding it wasn't worth what they were going through to live a little longer. That meant there was nine of us left, all of whom needed partners.

One by one we were called to Duke's office. Each anxious to meet our new partners.

The waiting was torture.

"You coming?" Emily asked from the doorway of the rest room, I jumped at the sound of her voice and looked up at her. "Duke's ready for you."

"Oh…"

"C'mon. You'll be ok." She gave me a comforting smile all I could do is nod and follow her to the office. Emily raised her hand to knock on the door, giving me another reassuring smile before leaving me to it.

"Come in." Duke's voice came through the door.

Tentatively I pushed open the door. "You wanted to see me sir?"

"Yes, please take a seat."

I nodded and moved to sit down on one of the chairs in front of his desk. Only then did I notice that the other was occupied. By Max.

Of course. It would be just my luck to be partnered with the sexist twat I met on my first day.

"Now." Duke began, eyes focusing on each of us in turn. "I'm sure you both know why you're here. Miss Barrett you have now completed your training and it is time you were assigned a partner. It is my belief that Mr Keen would be a good match."

"You have got to be kidding me." The words were out before I could stop them, luckily I wasn't the only one who was sceptical.

"With all due respect sir, I'm really not sure that's wise."

"And why would that be Mr Keen?" He asked, looking at Max over his glasses. Fixing him with a penetrating gaze.

"We had a clash of personalities within a few seconds of meeting each other…"

"What he's trying to say is if we work together we'd kill each other before anything else had a chance to."

"That's the point."

"What?" Max and I asked simultaneously.

"If you don't like each other you're going to be more aware of where the other is and what they're doing. Besides I'm sure that, given time, you'll come to get along quite well."

"I doubt that," I mumbled, not expecting to be overheard.

"Whether you believe it or not is irrelevant Miss Barrett. It's happening and that's the end of it. Now you both have the weekend off before you have to be in for your first assignment together. I suggest you use it to get to know each other."

"But sir, we don't have a single thing in common," Max stated, he was clutching at straws now.

"You have not wanting to work together in common. I suggest you work on that basis and move on from there."

"Please tell me this is some kind of joke."

"I'm afraid not Miss Barrett. Now if you'll excuse me, I do have work to attend to."

Out in the corridor, we stared at each other for a moment. In the end Max was the first to speak.

"I must admit, I am rather sceptical about the success of this venture."

"Yeah." I replied. "You and me both."

"I suppose we should do as we are instructed by our superior, so you are welcome to come back to my house."

I blinked at him for a moment. "Do you always talk like that?"

"Like what?"

"All posh and formal as if you think you're better than me."

"I'm dreadfully sorry. I never intended to cause offence. You also have my profuse apologies for when we first met. I now understand that my comment was considered sexist and rude."

I just blinked at him again before I came up with a response. "I guess that's ok. Emily did mention that you were struggling to adapt so no harm done I suppose."

"My most sincere gratitude."

"Anyway, we were going to your place?"

"Yes. I do need to locate the keys to my automobile beforehand though."

"OK. First things first, it's a car, Max. Please call it a car."

"I apologise." He caught sight of the side long look I gave him and quickly corrected himself. "I am sorry. I will try to remember in future."

"It's fine. Doesn't matter really."

On finally locating his keys we went to find his car. It was sleek and silver in design with tinted windows and looked like a cross between a rocket ship and an F1 car. He opened the passenger side door for me so I could see inside. The interior was decorated in black leathers and stained wood, the epitome of luxury.

"Wow," I whispered to myself.

"I know," he replied with a grin.

The rest of the journey to his flat was made in comfortable silence. It was only upon reaching his door that either of us spoke.

"Would you like a drink?" he asked, throwing his jacket over a coatrack on his way in.

"No, thank you." I carefully took off my own coat and hung it up, making sure it wouldn't get crumpled or creased.

As he went to make himself a drink I looked around the flat. The first thing to catch my attention was the large bay windows overlooking a cemetery. Once white gravestones littered the grass outside, taking up every possible centimetre of space. A Celtic cross stone was almost pressed against the window which Max seemed to have partially hidden behind potted plants. On the pristine white walls were various pieces of abstract artwork. A table sat in front of the windows surrounded by four striped chairs. The open plan design of the flat allowed me to see where he was retrieving a beer from the fridge. I was more than a little impressed, this was much more modern than I expected from a WWI soldier. I approached the CD player, I don't even know why there are still CD players, and started looking through the pile of CDs next to it.

"Would you care to put something on?" The sound of his voice made me jump.

"You like Bon Jovi?" I asked, admittedly somewhat accusingly.

"Of course. I believe that anyone with a working set of ears should be able to appreciate the works of Bon Jovi and Queen."

I stared at him for a moment, unsure of what to say. It's difficult to know how to react when someone you spent months hating admits they have the same taste in music. Finally my brain caught up with the programme. "You're making it very difficult to hate you right now."

His face lit up with the most beautifully sincere smile I've ever seen.

Wait.

I didn't just call him beautiful did I?

No of course I didn't that would be just absurd.

Rather than trying to think of something else to say I turned back to the CD player and put on my favourite song. As the first notes of 'What Do You Got?' began playing I asked the first question that came to my head. "Why do you have a CD player?"

The question seemed to take him somewhat off guard. "Excuse me?"

"The CD player. Surely two hundred years in the future it's gone the same way as the Phonograph or the tape player."

"Whilst for the most part it has, I rather like it." He explained, sitting down at the table and placing his beer down whilst never taking his eyes from me. "I found this one at an antiques shop and brought it home." As he spoke his cheeks seemed to flush red and his eyes slowly drifted towards his beer. "The CDs are so delicate and fragile they remind me that in life things must be cherished and preserved whilst you have them or you very well may regret it in the future."

"That is honestly the sappiest thing I've ever heard." In return for that comment I received a half smile. "Did you have any plans?"

"Excuse me?" He looks up at me slightly startled by the question.

"Before you died. Did you have any plans for the future?" As I asked the question I sat down on the chair next to him, my eyes never leaving his.

"Someday," he admitted softly. "Someday I wish to be married with a daughter named after my deceased mother."

"What was your mother's name?" I felt myself being drawn in but wasn't in any kind of position to stop it.

"Abigail."

"That's a beautiful name." I told him with a smile. "Maxwell and Abigail Keen. It's cute."

"Is… Is it something you have ever considered?" He asked, somewhat nervously.

"Once or twice. Maybe when I've been feeling particularly sentimental or melancholy I've wondered why I haven't found someone and whether there's just something fundamentally unlikable about me but… how can I find anyone when I don't even know what it is I actually want or am looking for?"

"I'm afraid I can't provide you with a reasonable or remotely helpful answer."

"It's alright Max, I didn't really expect you to."

~o~

*Temporal Tracers* is an extract from a novel, of the same name, I am currently in the process of writing. I wanted to experiment with a mixture of my two favourite genres: Romance and Science Fiction. The inspiration for the *Temporal Tracers* organisation is CI5 from the 1970s television series *The Professionals* and the corresponding 1990s remake, both of which are referenced within the story.

The story was originally started as a dare from my family to try writing something original rather than my usual kinds of transformative fiction. There are currently plans for a series of 4 books following Jessica's life in the 23rd Century.

A year ago I was diagnosed with a general anxiety disorder and I soon discovered the therapeutic nature of writing. It allows an escape from reality and a chance to create a world of my own that I can have complete control over which can be a great comfort during troublesome times.

I also believe that reading can have a similar effect. You hear countless stories of people who read a book that changed their lives for the better and that is what I would love to be able to do. If I could make a small difference to one person's life it would make the world that much better. Even if I do this through something as simple as providing a distraction and escape for the course of a book.

I don't know if I will ever become a professional writer but I would like to think it possible and the *Temporal Tracers* marks a first real attempt to make this dream a reality. It allowed me to realise that what I had once considered a far flung hope may actually have a chance at coming to pass.

# DAVID KRAJNYAK
## CENSORSHIP

David Krajnyak was born in Hungary, however, he moved to Britain to pursue a university degree of English Literature and Creative Writing in Aberdeen. He won several writing competitions during his early high school years, having published poems and short stories. Although, his most important success was the publication of an original collection of short stories in 2013 back home in Hungary, which was also followed by media appearances! He has been writing privately in English for more than five years, however, he now felt ready to a first attempt for an official publication in the language. He hopes to become a secondary teacher of English Literature, also aiming to fulfil his wishes of being a playwright, novelist or screenwriter.

*There is war ~~and corruption~~. Why should we hide facts? I was asked to write and I accepted because ~~I had no other choice not because~~ I wanted to speak up. People believe in me, I am one of the few who are left with credit. ~~I would lie if I said that~~ everything is alright. This might be dangerous to say but I have to come out with this statement. People die for our ~~corrupt and devastated~~ country - this is ~~more pathetic and horrible than~~ heroic. Our enemies are attacking ~~a fascist government, they are not targeted against~~ us, they do ~~not~~ want to kill us, they want to kill our ~~horrendous~~ ideology. An ideology that resulted in ~~the death of~~ millions ~~believing they were~~ fighting for liberty. And here it is, a country without a future - ~~is that~~ the liberty you all wanted?. And*

## David Krajnyak

*here is me ~~left standing~~, ~~the last living~~ member of the ~~formerly numerous~~ opposition kept alive ~~as a puppet~~, ~~as a lunatic who~~ is telling the truth that everybody ~~laughs at and noone~~ believes in. ~~When will people~~ believe me?! It was hard to me to write it down, ~~because I know~~ as the biggest critic of the government ,~~I will be executed now~~. They are ~~not~~ right on this war, ~~executions won't make them right~~! ~~Refuse to~~ fight! I know that my words ~~most probably~~ will ~~not~~ reach you. I ~~just~~ want the future, ~~if there is any slight chance~~, to know that ~~there was~~ someone ~~who~~ fought for a cause!*

*David Porter*

*Note from editor: some passages were crossed out because they reveal the location and plans of the national government - for security reasons they have been removed. Enjoy the encouraging speech of David Porter, leader of the opposition! Join all forces now for a better future!*

The wind carried a piece of paper - it was silent now, only this gentle motion of nature affected the solitude of the city. As the first leaflet got caught on a cobweb many more seemed to arrive with the wind. A symphony of whistling, blowing and light cracking, it was music to the ears of the people who haven't heard anything but cannons and bombs in the past decade. Cautiously, a middle-aged man walked out of a destructed house and picked up the leaflet. He read it shaking his head and wearing a concerned expression on his face as he entered his home.

'Do you believe this, Dorothy?' he asked doubtfully from a woman sitting in the dusty and rusty kitchen after he gave the paper to her.

'Doesn't sound like him' - she added, now reading the piece of paper. 'You know him Arch, you should know.'

'If he wrote this, I don't know him anymore.'

While they were discussing the leaflet, roaring sounds became more and more strong outside in the middle of the district. Arch slowly approached the window and glanced out. He saw some of his neighbours assembling on the main square.

'He has spoken out!' - shouted one of them - 'We should go to war!'

'If he said so, we must go fight indeed' - said another. - 'Enough of hiding! End this bloody war!'

'Can't you see through this, Jake?' shouted a strongly built, but very short man 'Just because his name is written on it why do you believe it's him?'

'He always criticized the leader!' replied the first man.

'He could always get away with his opinion. This is our time now! If we cooperate, things will turn out for the best! Maybe even elections after we win!' added the second advocate.

'Something is terribly wrong here, don't believe this! They killed most of our wives last time to make us miserable. They spared our life just to leave us suffer! They let us run to make us disgraced. It's our turn now, they want to hunt us down, why would they tolerate us any more?'

More and more men joined the argument. Slowly weapons were uncovered from hidden, dust-covered boxes and a large group of men accumulated ready to leave.

'Where are you going?' asked Dorothy 'You don't believe in this, do you?'

'I don't!' said Arch, and started to write on a piece of paper 'But whatever this might mean, one thing is for sure: all hope is gone. One way or another we lost. We have to go. To heaven or hell, I don't know.'

A group of a thousand men and some dozen women fully armoured started to march. The rest who decided to stay at home quickly fled, closed the windows and shutters and hid in their basements.

The roar was inhuman. Paced perfectly simultaneously, a thousand marched towards the capital city to join forces with the dictator. A thousand rebels now following order of one person they believed in, though they knew they could never properly hear what he was trying to say. Leaving the city, while the march started to cross an abandoned, contaminated field, massive planes appeared on the sky. Their number was innumerable, the sun started to fade. Arch stopped and put the paper he wrote back in the house in a strong metallic box. He quit the marching people and started to dig in the ground. Some shouted at him, some continued to march but the unity was dissipating as they experienced the darkness coming. When the bombs started to fall he covered the piece of land where he dug with his body and closed his eyes.

*Two hundred years later*

The sun shone on a world that was having no alternative. Not any more. Destructed and decayed houses, bones everywhere, and the wind... The wind that carries a single paper, a symphony of cracking and smooth whistling that noone hears.

*Enemy, or our very own people? Both in one, one in both? We don't know. But we had to go. All I know is that we can't even trust the ones we have common enemy with. Not even our senses, not even ourselves. A world like this does not deserve survival. I could've loved, if I had the chance. Thank you Dorothy. Maybe, in a later time there will be a second chance. For now, it's only to perish.*

~o~

I have long been interested in manipulation, falsification and representation of statistical data. Everything we read is written from a certain point of view that is influenced by factors such as politics, ideologies, personal beliefs, etc... Sometimes I have a feeling that we cannot trust any resources because some people are so willing to prove their truth (i.e. unjustified belief) that they do not deter from falsifying data or present it in a way that it appeals to them. Let's say I want to prove that strawberries are better than raspberries. I am going to make interviews with people and only going to present the answers that justify me and neglect or suppress the significance of the raspberry fans. Or let's say I am a minister of economics and would like to prove that my country did very well with their 0.01% GDP growth this year. To achieve this, I focus on the period of a month on a graph where growth was 2% and talk hours about how well we did in July, compared to the previous government who made losses in last July, not mentioning gross data. Therefore, we have to be very cautious about information: who says it, what is it good for, what does it represent, who profits from it? The list could go on forever. In this writing I wanted to represent the importance of information and how we read it!

# ELLIE PAYNE
## LESSER OF TWO EVILS

Ellie Payne is a nineteen-year-old student, originally from Nottinghamshire. She is currently reading Creative Writing at Sheffield Hallam University and only began sharing her writing with others last year. *Lesser of Two Evils* is her first published piece and she hopes it won't be the last. When she isn't writing, Ellie enjoys reading a wide array of genres and finding interesting spoken word poetry.

It was as though Dementia had stalked my father for all of his seventy-two years, waiting for a moment of weakness to pounce; the injured runt of the herd, ripe for the picking. The day Mum died, Dad stumbled and Dementia leapt, dragging him to the ground. Unlike a zebra trapped in the lion's jaw, there was no struggle from Dad, no fight to survive. For two years they were locked in an impasse, disease vs man. Dementia didn't have the mercy to kill, while Dad no longer had the resolve to care. At a time when we should have been united in grief, fighting off an army of well-meaning busybodies forcing their condolences and offerings of food upon us, we were battling to get through to our dad.

I arrived early one particular morning, trailing snow with me as I slammed the door, cursing the terrible weather as I breezed through the living room and into the kitchen. It wasn't until I stood watching the steam swirling up from the second mug of tea that I realised there was a significant figure missing.

That was the first of two suicide attempts, both foiled by the adult daughters who refused to be orphans. His increasingly frail body had been limp and cold on the bed, but with the faintest breath still left in his body, he was rushed to hospital. Both times he asked 'Why?' and we'd reply, 'Because we love you.' Because we're selfish. Because we needed him to make us feel whole.

❖

"There you go, Dad, a fresh mug of tea." My wide smile was almost deranged. All I got in return was a grunt as he slowly made his way through a family photo album. I set the new mug down beside him, removing its untouched predecessor.

I had arrived that morning to find him at the dining table surrounded by photo albums, staring into faces with a frown. He hadn't spoken more than a few syllables to me since I'd arrived. "Our Sandra will be here soon to cook you a nice dinner - shall we move these out the way, maybe move to the lounge?" I said.

He waved me away with another grunt and hunched closer to the page. I leant back with a sigh, crossing my arms and counting the minutes until my sister would arrive to relieve me. I desperately missed the cushy adult daughter role.

"Aunty Carol," he suddenly declared proudly, tapping a finger on her face. I smiled at him, nodding with too much enthusiasm. "She's in San Francisco now."

The smile dropped. His sister had died a lengthy death courtesy of ovarian cancer seven years before. How was I supposed to correct him and make him face the loss all over again? I remained silent and picked up a photo album of my own. The first page in the album featured Mum on her fiftieth birthday. She beamed at the camera, the restaurant's linen napkin tucked into the neckline of her best blouse in a snapshot that entirely summed up my mum, lacking in refinement but full of warmth and kindness. I paused on the page.

"Who's that lady?"

My head snapped up to look at Dad. I hadn't noticed him craning over to look but he now hovered over my shoulder wearing a deep frown. Rage built up, hot against the nape of my neck, poking tiny pins against my skin.

Forgetting the date was one thing, but to forget the woman he had been in love with since he was eighteen was sacrilege. I knew dementia. I knew that he couldn't be held accountable for such lapses, but this knowledge did nothing to dispel the anger I found directed at my father.

"Hello, only me!" Sandra's sweet voice rang out, accompanied by the rustle of shopping bags as she clattered through the back door.

I glanced at Dad and found him frozen. His eyes slid up to mine and filled with tears.

"I forgot her," he whispered. "My Marjorie."

Sandra entered with a beaming smile, already tying an apron around her waist. "How does pie and mash sound, Dad?"

"Great, love," he croaked. Sandra smiled at him and nodded for me to follow her back into the kitchen. I had begun to rise, only for Dad to put his hand over mine with a surprisingly strong grip.

"I won't be a minute," I called, dropping back into the seat with a thump. He withdrew his hands and they rose to his head with a will of their own before making a shaky, exploratory journey over his skull, as though feeling for the source of the problem, possibly a simple puncture that was to blame for the monstrous way his memories had been betraying him.

"This is no life." His voice trembled with the first real emotion I'd seen from him for some time. His clenched fist came down on the table, in a somewhat pathetic punch.

"Oh no, come on," I objected feebly, unable to offer a pragmatic argument. "You have Sandra and me."

"You are my children. You have no business taking on the burden of caring for me in the way you have been," he muttered, resembling a sullen child. "I'm supposed to care for you."

"You did care for us. We couldn't have wanted more from you."

"Well now I want something."

I had become so accustomed to blank stares and long silences that his sharpness was unsettling.

"Anything. Except-"

"I want out." His stare's penetrative power was matched only by the suffocating silence that accompanied it.

" Anything but that."

"You don't understand!" His voice was weak, desperate.

"You're right, I don't understand why you keep putting me in this position."

It was after the second of the suicide attempts. He had held on tight to my hand, his bony fingers digging in painfully as I made to draw away from the hospital bed. He had begged, in rasping whispers, for my help but he had spooked me and I left in a fit of tears. I didn't visit him, even once he had returned home, for a month.

"I'm no good to anyone like this." Tears had begun to drip from his whiskered chin. "I hate that I have to do this to you. It will be the last time I am a burden. Please."

"What about Sandra?" I suggested out of desperation.

"No love, I need your help. You know what our Sandra is like, too emotional to think this through."

"She'd hate me," I argued. "If I did this for you, you'd be leaving me all alone. I need you."

I rose from the table, glad he didn't try to stop me again. Instead, as I made my way to the kitchen he stared after me looking heartbroken.

"Finally!" Sandra scolded as I entered. She was enthusiastically rubbing butter into her dough mixture. "How has he been?"

"Fine," I replied, my mind still ringing with Dad's request.

"You're about as talkative as Dad," she laughed. "He was at the doctor's on Tuesday and they said he's lost quite a bit of weight and that we need to encourage him to eat as much as possible. I've made him a meal plan for the week so if you stick to that we should be alright. Has he eaten much today?"

She kept up a constant stream of chatter as she manned the kitchen with an irritating level of competence. After this she would return to her spotless four bedroom home to cook a nourishing and homely meal for her family. Unlike me, hopelessly out of my depth nursing an ill old man, Sandra was in her element as a Florence Nightingale figure.

"He ate a couple of hard boiled eggs earlier," I replied when she finally left a gap in the conversation.

"Mandy, you have to make him eat," she scolded.

"What do you expect me to do? Feed him up like a Foie Gras duck?"

"We have to keep his morale up, and people are happy when they eat," Sandra snapped, before she dropped the dough onto the counter with a thud and had at it with the rolling pin.

"Not when they're suicidal."

She whirled around and tore the potato and knife from me, the peel swaying perilously as she waved her hands around "He isn't suicidal. He's just sad and has every right to be. But he has us and we *will* make his last years happy and filled with love." The sweet sentiments of her speech were somewhat ruined by the knife she wielded.

"Years?" I snapped. "You mean the *decade* the doctor told us to expect Dad to trudge on for? Do you really think Dad will want to live like this for another ten years?"

"Do you not want every moment possible with him? Or is him being ill too much of an inconvenience for you?" She asked.

"I have 34 years of happy memories with him, I don't need to squeeze every last second of time with him. If I'm honest, these past two years have marred the happier times"

Memories of winter afternoons baking side by side in this very kitchen flooded back, a time when food brought the family together. But food had become a source of frustration, a daily struggle with Dad.

"Our Dad is battling a debilitating illness and you're only worried about your memories?" Sandra laughed. "You mean the memories where you're his little baby without a care in the world? You're so selfish."

"Battle?" I had to catch myself before our conversation rose above hisses, but the scorn was difficult to control. "Don't ennoble Dementia like that. You make it sound as though it's an evenly matched fight. A battle involves a certain amount of honour but what Dad has fallen victim to is unscrupulous."

"What a grand speech." Sandra adopted the same infuriating tone she'd used on me my entire life "While you're apparently quite good at speeches, you should leave the medicine to the professionals. Doctor Reynolds told us Dad will live for ten years, so we make them comfortable and happy for him."

"Oh yes, the medical professionals who just give idiotic people like you false hope, while they drag out the demise of our loved ones for the sake of upholding their unconscionable Hippocratic Oath!"

"The Hippocratic Oath is designed to protect patients." Her patronising tone only served to increase my frustration at her unwillingness to accept the truth.

"No it isn't! All they're doing is blindly preserving life without thought for quality, when it would be in the patient's best interest to die."

"That's an evil thing to say," Sandra spat. "I think you should leave. I don't want someone who isn't dedicated to Dad caring for him."

"He's not even really Dad anymore. He's basically an empty shell and is completely miserable." I told her as I shoved my arms through my coat.

"So because he's not fun anymore you think we should abandon him? After all he did for us growing up, you don't think he's worth saving?"

"Not abandon him, just stop treating each new illness or problem as it comes up and let nature take its course. There is no point in plugging up holes in a sinking ship."

"Get out," she said contemptuously, not even bothering to look at me as I left.

I waited outside for three hours after Sandra and I argued, carefully considering my options. When Dad had first asked the unthinkable of me, I had been horrified, but the more I thought about it, the more I saw from his perspective. During the time I had kept away I had been drawn to research. The next time Dad asked, I wanted to be ready. Though I had stumbled earlier, letting my emotions take over, I was ready now.

Considering she was only supposed to be making some dinner, Sandra had taken a long time to leave the house. I pictured her reading Dad's letters and sorting them into piles, checking everything was turned off and locked, generally fussing around.

When she finally appeared on the doorstep, she was teetering under the weight of a cardboard box. I strained to see what it could possibly contain, but it was quickly deposited into the boot of her car and the door swiftly slammed shut.

I watched her car grow further and further away and then got out, leaving my own car a short distance from the house. I walked round to the back door and let myself back into the small kitchen.

The house was shadowy and hushed as I selected one of the firm feather cushions from the sofa and made for the hallway just off of the living room. As I passed the dresser, the niggling feeling that the familiar landscape of its cluttered contents had been altered, though hastily rearranged, resolved itself into a conviction.

It only took a second for me to realise that several items had been removed, most noticeably a commemorative tankard, marking twenty-five years of Dad's loyal service to Layman's Brewery.

Despite all Sandra's hot air about Dad living a long and happy life, it appeared that the hypocrite was already staking her claim to all of the best heirlooms. This was not entirely unexpected, since after Mum's death Sandra had taken to swanning around in our mother's favourite pearls and sniffling in a heartfelt manner if she was ever challenged about it. Well, she could have the dusty old mug. I was planning to give Dad the ultimate gift.

I would let her painstakingly pick out the flowers and music and have everyone agree in hushed tones about how saint-like she was, because I would have carried out a great act of human kindness. I would be the better daughter, selflessly putting my own feelings aside to assist a soul in distress.

The door creaked as I pushed it open, revealing Dad's bedroom, cast with a purple hue as artificial light shone through the thin curtains, making Dad no more than a dark lump in the centre of the bed. Sneaking into our parents' sanctuary provoked eerie memories of Christmas mornings as a child, Sandra and I hand in hand; a temporary truce declared for the sake of Santa.

I approached slowly, navigating the creaky floorboards like a minefield. I lingered, the cushion inches above his head. I sucked in a deep breath and finally built up the courage to bring it down over his face.

My slow counting was interrupted by an odd sensation between my fingers, warm and wet. I thought back through the articles I had read and none of them mentioned a liquid of any kind. Lifting the cushion cautiously, expecting dad to jerk up, I found dark stains on both sides of the cushion.

Horror and fury had simultaneously ripped through me as I slowly turned him, revealing a large, ugly gash on his forehead, blood flowing down his face and onto his pyjama top. My thoughts immediately turned to violent robbery.

But, Sandra had been in the house the entire time I had waited outside. She hadn't looked particularly flustered or nervous upon leaving, but then again she'd always had the perfect poker face. I didn't find it hard to believe that such a ruthless woman would be capable of murder, it was her chosen victim that highlighted a hole in my theory. Why, when she had devoted so much time and attention to caring for him, would she brutally murder our father?

I fished my phone from my coat pocket and backed from the room, pulling the door shut quietly, as though to avoid waking him and hurried to the back door. I looked around the neighbouring gardens, cloaked by the darkness of night which had set in, and then rushed for my car. My cold fingers at first refused to cooperate with me as I searched through my contacts, looking for Sandra's number.

The phone rang for longer than Sandra would usually allow. Finally there was a click and she came onto the line.

"What have you done?" I demanded, cutting off her breezy greeting.

"You're going to need to be more specific," she began. "I stopped by the supermarket on my way home-"

"I'm referring to the fact that you have battered our father's brains in, then left him lying in his own blood for me to find."

She spluttered, "Are you telling me Dad has been murdered?" I could hear her trying to work up tears and emotion.

"Oh, stop it, Sandra. I can always tell when you're lying, I knew when you sneaked boys into your room and I know that you're a murderer. I want to know why?. Why Dad?"

"You always accuse me of being cold, yet you don't seem particularly distraught yourself." Her voice was back to her usual crisp tone.

"That'll be because I've already come to terms with Dad's death on account of how I have been planning to help him die with some dignity. Like he asked."

Sandra barked out a laugh "Lucky old Dad, two murderous daughters."

"I'm only murderous with the best of intents. What drove Florence Nightingale to this?" I gloated.

"Money," she sighed.

"But what happened to spending every last moment with him and your precious 'years to come'?"

"I got a call from my solicitor while I was finishing dinner. Dad isn't of sound mind and can't sign any legal documents. Just my luck."

Sandra had always hidden this side of herself from our parents, having them convinced that she was a little darling, but as a little sister you get to know the depth of depravity to which your sibling can stoop.

"And what exactly did you plan to do? Convince Dad to sign over everything to you and leave me with nothing? Does Richard not give you enough pocket money to keep up with the other yummy mummies?" I mocked.

"Richard has got himself, and by default me, into massive debt and we can barely afford to keep the house. We're behind on Thomas' school payments and I've had to buy a DIY highlighting kit"

"The horror," I said.

"Quite. The real problem, now that you know, is where do we go from here?"

"I tell the police that you're a murderer, prison eases your money worries and I come into a larger than expected inheritance."

"You're such a bad bluffer. Fine, I'll give you your share," Sandra said casually, as though she was doing me a favour.

"You're missing the point here," I laughed, enjoying my power over the girl who had always pulled my hair and manipulated me. "Why would I take a measly half when I could take everything?"

"For the same reason I no longer can. We both know too much."

A silence followed as we both considered our options. Sandra's mind would have been working a mile a minute, no doubt retracing all of her actions to see if there was the smallest chance she could involve me, her instincts like a trapped wild animal; take out your captor or die trying.

Sandra broke first "You say the two of you had plotted an assisted suicide… what do the logistics matter? He's at peace and we're still here. He would want us to protect ourselves"

"At peace? Sandra, you smashed his brains in!"

"But it's done! Dad isn't suffering anymore. Now we need to think about *our* futures. You need to be mature enough to accept that this whole situation could be beneficial for both of us, without any… ugliness."

❖

## Ellie Payne

And so it began, the secret that binds Sandra and me together in a grizzly pact of silence, mutual distrust and façade.

The hunt for the violent thugs that ransacked our father's home before murdering him in his bed produced no conclusive evidence and was eventually filed as a cold case. During the investigation we grieved in the headlines for a few weeks before the eyes of Britain found a new case to follow.

At least I can rest easy in the knowledge that I am the lesser of two evils.

~o~

The idea for *Lesser of Two Evils* came from a discussion I had about my late Grandad, who had struggled with Dementia, and how he would have felt if he had known his fate. This conversation took place around the same time a story was in the news about the right to die and these combined factors created an idea that I worked on for several months. I have always enjoyed books which explore controversial topics and always want my writing to have a greater meaning which grips the reader and encourages debate. Peer feedback confirmed that the main character in my piece introduces conflict within the reader, leaving them unsure whether they should like her or not, which was part of my goal. I also enjoy plots that aren't neatly tied up at the end and surprise the reader, which is why I chose to let the sisters get away with their crime, instead choosing to leave the omniscient narrator role for a moment and share the outside perspective of a cold case and mourning daughters.

No singular author directly inspired this piece, however, in general, Katherine Mansfield is inspiring to me. I hope to one day be able to replicate her ability to build up a story through seemingly inconsequential moments. Malorie Blackman is another author whom I greatly admire, particularly the *Noughts and Crosses* series, for her ability to spark discussion within a dystopia setting, in which the reader doesn't even necessarily realise their perspective is being challenged.

Upon leaving university I would like to have at least one more piece published. Writing fiction for a living is my ultimate goal, however I know the likelihood of reaching JK Rowling heights is low. A role in marketing for a charity is my planned safety net job.

# ANDREW HEALEY
## FRESHWATER LOVER

Andrew Healey is a twenty-three-year-old writer. He grew up in Sevenoaks and then moved to London, where he studies on the Creative Writing BA program at Birkbeck, University of London. He tweets @healeywrites, and is working on his first novel. *Freshwater Lover* is his first publication.

Our little Bloomsbury flat is *not* on fire from the outside. It was probably an empty threat.

Inside, there isn't any crying, and strangely, nothing seems smashed. "Kevin?" I call out. The bathroom door is shut and I knock. "You in there—pal?" I ask, opting for a neutral nickname but it comes out odd-sounding.

I open the door. It's humid inside. Kevin is lying in the bathtub, water up to his neck. His ears are submerged and he gives me a look. "What's up?" he asks a little too loud.

"Just checking on you," I say, using my hand to cover his penis from my eye-line.

He looks away.

I head to the kitchen.

There are no tea bags. I google: living with an ex. I idly scan a gif-scattered listicle. I watch Patrick Bateman getting ready to swing an axe at Paul Allen on loop.

I take the first formal step. I log onto Netflix and disconnect all devices. Kevin and I were watching Breaking Bad together, but now, on the couch, I load up the next episode without him. I lower the volume though, so he can't hear spoilers from the bathroom.

I wake in the dark and need to pee. I sit on the loo and stare at floating Kevin.

I have an intrusive thought: the police question me out in the hall, asking just how my ex-boyfriend managed to drown in the apartment with me in the next room. His mother wails in the background.

"Wake up," I say.

"Why?" He doesn't open his eyes. "You can have the bed."

"And where are you going to sleep?"

He lifts out a wrinkly hand and points down at the bath.

"Right then," I tell him as I wipe.

The bed smells like us. I turn over trying to remember the comfort it used to bring.

Someone is knocking on the door. I make my way there with my dressing gown half on. "Hello?" I offer as I tuck my left boob in.

"Open up," Kevin's mum says.

"Oh hi, Marie."

"Don't *Hi Marie* me. Where is he?" she asks, pushing past me. "Kevin?"

I shrug to no one and return to bed, wrapping my pillow around my head. There's a dirty bowl on the floor. Under the bits of food there are childlike flowers that we painted onto the bowl and had glazed during better times.

There are loud footsteps and I roll over. "Ugh," she says.

"What's up?" I slur. My left boob slips free.

"Really?" she gestures. "I don't know what you did to him but—"

"I didn't do anything, we broke up."

"You broke him, so you need to fix this." She jabs at me, and turns, muttering about the bath.

Work is busy. A boy comes in to complain that his sandwich isn't toasted enough. "It's just moist!" he says, staring at me and then down at the sweaty BLT.

On my way back, I see an advert on the side of a bus: a man in trunks diving into clear tropical water.

I stand over Kevin at home. "How are we going to do this?" I ask. He's doing that thing again where his ears are underwater.

"You sound like whale-song."

"Don't try and be deep."

"*Deep*—good one," he says.

"Fuck off."

I leave some cans and a tin opener on the bathmat.

I wonder if I pushed him into this somehow. Yes, my breakup speech ended up blurring into clichés but how else do you define *lack of spark*?

I check on him in the morning and he's sleeping like an upturned gator: his pruning belly rising and falling. The water lapping softy at his sides.

Kevin's phone won't stop ringing. I pick it up and it's the cinema where he works. They ask where the hell he's been and I mumble something about a family bereavement. *What?* the voice at the other end of the line says. I mumble again, quieter this time, and hang up.

It's been two weeks. I call the police to the apartment, using the phrase *erratic behaviour*.

Disinterested, two officers arrive. "He's in there of his own free will," the burly one says. "Has he made any threats to your person? Or himself?" His partner is staring out the kitchen window and mutters something about human rights. I shake my head.

Unsure what else to do, I start a twitter account for him. @KevinSoaks. A freshwater biologist messages me and says it's a goldmine for academic study.

The edges of Kevin's face are peeling—along with everything else. His penis looks like a pale gherkin covered in brine gunk.

The biologist comes around to take a sample.

"Albert," I ponder out loud, "why did you choose freshwater over marine biology?"

"Marine biologists think they're rock stars." He dips a tube into the water. "It all goes to their heads."

"Are you two sleeping together?" Kevin shouts, submerged.

"No," I lie.

Albert takes me out for a pizza and talks about Kevin. I fail to steer the conversation towards anything else. I get the feeling he's using me.

"Wait, how are you even going to the loo?" I ask Kevin one day.

"What?" he asks, sticking a fluffy finger into his underwater ear to clear it. Some of the cartilage is showing. I notice the cans I left are still on the bathmat.

I get scared.

Albert keeps texting me water-based puns so I block him.

I get frustrated at Kevin and throw a shampoo bottle at his head. Part of his scalp lifts up and the water near that end goes a cloudy red. His lips are the only part of him that aren't waxy and waterlogged. They're pink and they part and let out a soft, "Please?" It's a gentle voice I haven't heard in years.

I kneel and reach down for his fraying hand. It's spongy and I squeeze it. "I'm sorry," I say, "about all of this. And I did sleep with Albert but he was dick."

"It's okay. I'm not perfect either." He opens his eyes underwater and looks at me. All around the pupils his eyes are bright red.

"Can I get you anything?" I ask.

We're interrupted by a knock on the door. I let go of Kevin's hand. He tries to hold onto me but he's too weak.

"Open up!" his mother shouts. There's more than one voice in the hallway. I open the door a crack and she barges past. "I've come for my son." She's followed by Albert and two assistants in hospital scrubs.

"What are you doing?" I rush to block them from the bathroom.

"Get out of our way," she commands. The assistants are wheeling in a pale blue, latex hammock. Albert looks on proudly. I turn to look at Kevin. His bottom lip vibrates in the water. Tiny ripples around his mouth. She shoves my shoulder and I fall and crack my elbow against the floor.

Albert kneels down and I flinch back from him. Kevin's mother rips out the plug and I yell: "You're washing him away!"

The assistants scoop his slimy, skeletal body into the hammock. Albert blocks the apartment door until they're all the way outside. I look down at the street from my window and scream. I go to the bath and put the furry plug back in. The sides are lined with pink mush and tiny little hairs. As I step in, my feet squish down against the bottom. I slide into the bath, scratching my back on the hard lumps of Kevin coral. I spin both taps open. I whisper: "I'm coming, baby. I'm coming."

~o~

Lately, I've been interested in exploring the anxiety of separation, internet culture, and mental illness. In a way, this story hits all three. It's about a modern breakup where someone doesn't take it so well.

Breakups can be scary. I've found that they feel like a daydream. You're walking around making decisions but it doesn't really feel like you're there. It's like you've come back from being on holiday. Except you've come back beaten, confused, and now you've been given more responsibilities, like feeding and dressing yourself, which never felt like things you had to force yourself to do before. It's a surreal time, so I wanted to push this in my story, while keeping the trappings of modern life: gifs, Netflix, Twitter.

Breakups feel temporary until you get the pang that they're permanent. I wanted to show this by removing a process the body goes though: the ability to unwrinkle itself. Pruney fingers were a mystery to me growing up. In just ten minutes, your hands can look as old as your grandparent's. I chose to make Kevin undergo this change permanently.

Lately, I've been really into short punchy paragraphs, and the way writing is presented online with line breaks instead of paragraphs. I love this style, I think it's much easier to read and it's definitely influenced this story. In the lead up to writing this piece, I had been gorging myself on online literary magazines.

I think writing fiction is one of the best ways to reach out to people who are scared about the way they are living their lives, particularly when it comes to the rise of people experiencing anxiety disorders. I draw on my own experience of mental illness in order to empathise with my reader and create believable characters and situations.

# CHRISTINA FOSTER
## NOT A FAIRY TALE

Christina Foster is twenty-one years old and from Burnley, England. She is currently in her second year reading psychology at the University of Central Lancashire. She has written a novella that she hopes will be published someday, and has previously had a poem published. She also enjoys reading and playing video games.

Once upon a time, a brave prince was destined to be king. He was strong and well liked but he didn't have a queen, so he set out to find a deserving woman. He told all his best men to scout out such a woman, and a few days later one came back with a story of a damsel in distress.

The beloved prince learned that an evil old hag had locked up a young woman in a tall, dark tower. This woman was not a witch because this is not a fairy tale.

The prince could think of no one better than this mysterious damsel; the villagers said she had the beauty of an angel, which was an added bonus.

She was trapped and scared and he would be her saviour.

That very day the prince mounted his graceful stallion in a rather ungraceful way due to his heavy steel armour, and raced to the tower.

He galloped over his many luscious and productive fields, shouting greetings to his loyal subjects as he passed. He stopped only to accept a glass of fresh cool milk from a farmer's wife who had hurried out when she saw him coming.

Soon however, the green grass became dark murky paths and there was nobody around. Even the air felt chillier, but this must have just been his imagination, the prince chastised himself. A few minutes later he rounded a corner and before him stood a huge gloomy looking castle guarded by uninviting and rather foreboding looking gates. Being a brave prince though, he charged through them with no hesitation and dismounted.

The castle was enormous. It had huge wooden doors at the front and there was a tower at each of its four corners, connected to the main building by a stone bridge.

To the prince's delight, he spotted the beautiful prisoner at the top window of the north tower. Quickly, he removed his helmet and neatened his dark brown hair, before shouting, "Fair lady let down your hair!"

But this is not a fairy tale so the young woman did not hear him and definitely did not let him attempt to climb her hair.

The prince stood still for a moment deciding what to do next until he spotted a few stones by his feet. He gathered a few and taking careful aim, threw one towards the window to gain the damsel's attention. The stone flew up through the air higher and higher until . . . It fell back down several meters from the window. This is not a fairy tale and the prince was not a master of sport.

However, he was determined so pulled out his trusty slingshot and loaded it. Seconds later he watched as the stone flew towards the window. It went further than the first stone but still fell short.

Not perturbed, the prince optimistically aimed a third stone. This time the small missile flew higher and higher... and directly through the open window, hitting the back of the damsel's head, who collapsed unconscious. After all, stones are hard and this is not a fairy tale.

The prince watched in dismay before deciding that it was now even more important that he reach the prisoner to make sure she was unhurt..

Cautiously, he headed toward the dark eerie castle, which was surrounded by thick greenery. What could be awaiting him in all those shrubs? It sent shivers down his spine but he had to reach the door behind. Still, there could be a mighty dragon? A fearsome tiger? He was 99% sure dragons only existed in fairy tales. Besides which, the bush was much too small to cover one.

So the prince happily ruled out that fearsome beast of legend. Tigers however, were another problem; the prince knew they definitely did exist but was quite certain, or hoped, that none existed in his country of Albia.

Nervously, he prodded the bush with a sharp stick and let out a high-pitched yelp as something caught onto it. He dropped the stick and sprinted through the greenery and towards the entrance door certain that he could hear fierce tiger roars close behind him.

Within seconds, he reached the huge wooden castle door, which to his surprise were unlocked, and slammed it closed behind him before promptly collapsing against the other side sweating heavily but barely daring to breathe in case the tiger should hear him.

When finally the prince had regathered his courage, he pulled himself up and bravely looked out of a nearby window. He couldn't believe what he saw: by the bush, was an adorable kitten rolling around and playing with the stick he had dropped in panic. Could that have scared him? No, he consoled himself; he was a brave prince of Albia who often had to fight to protect his beloved country so no harmless animal could have scared him. The tiger must have fled and then the kitten ventured out of its hiding place where it had no doubt been hiding in terror. He made a mental note to inform his men of the escaped tiger, which ought to be hunted down to protect the villagers.

As he moved away from the window, he felt something soft brush against his head. Fighting the urge to shriek once again, he quickly pulled out a torch from his pocket and shone it up to reveal a spider's web. He stepped away from the window and scanned the cold, dark room. Cobwebs hung haphazardly around it, the only light being from his torch. The floors and walls were made of jagged stone, both were dark but there was a hint of paler colours in the floor suggesting it was darkened with age and dirt. The room contained little furniture, only a moth eaten sofa and a rotting wooden table.

Carefully the prince made his way across the room towards a door on the opposite side. He pulled on the handle but the door stayed firmly closed. Luckily, for the prince however, on closer inspection he noticed the wood surrounding the lock was rotten. He searched his pockets and eventually pulled out a sharp penknife, which he used to cut out the old lock; it fell to the floor with a small thud. The door was still stiff and took all of the prince's strength to force it open. It creaked loudly in protest but finally revealed the next room. Soon the prince was rapidly making his way through room after room of old abandoned furniture. Everything was neat, as if the owner would return at any minute.

Bravely he continued on his quest and opened the next door. On the other side was a huge, spiral staircase. It was made of white marble and so tall that the prince could not see the top. After taking a deep breath, he started the long climb.

Eventually the prince reached a door and pushed it open. He found himself in an abandoned corridor. He made his way through it, opening doors on either side, hoping to find a way to the damsel's tower but he had no luck. That is, until he reached a tall door at the very end of the corridor.

He was nearly knocked off his feet by a huge gust of wind as soon as he opened the door but caught onto a nearby chair. Then unluckily for the prince ancient dust was stirred up in the room causing him to cough violently.

When he had recovered, he looked back through the door to see if it could lead him forwards in his valiant quest. Outside he saw a stone bridge high above the ground that despite its strong material appeared rickety and unsafe. This did not improve his confidence because although he was a brave prince who had fought in many wars, this is not a fairy-tale, and even valiant princes have fears. This prince's fear was an uncontrollable anxiety about heights. His legs shook as he stepped onto the bridge and he grabbed a small stone wall, which lined both sides, for support. Slowly he edged along the bridge toward a couple of steps leading up to another wooden door. It was a slow process as the prince was terrified he would fall at any moment but he managed to reach the door at last.

Unsure of what he would see on the other side, he opened it slowly. He was completely unprepared for what he saw. All the rooms he had been through so far were old, dirty and abandoned, but he was now presented with a sparklingly clean corridor. There was no dust and they were even pictures hung up along the wall.

'The damsel will have nothing else to do but clean so this makes perfect sense,' the prince reasoned to himself.

He started his search for the unconscious damsel.

# Not A Fairy Tale

Noticing how smoothly the doors now opened compared to the others, the prince opened the first one to reveal an elegantly furnished room. He wondered where the damsel would have got all the clean furniture from but decided this was not the time to ponder about trivial things.

A cream coloured sofa faced a reasonably sized television. This might seem out of place, but remember, this is not a fairy tale ince quickly noticed the broken window on the opposite side of the bed, so jumped over to greet his to-be princess. Sure enough, she was lying just below the window completely still. She had smooth, light coloured hair and her skin was soft to the touch. She wore a long, dark blue dress that was decorated with small jewels and she was undoubtedly the most beautiful woman the prince had ever seen. He knew exactly what to do: he leaned down and gently kissed her soft lips. Her beautiful blue eyes slowly blinked open to twinkling in the light.

"Fair lady, I have come to rescue you. You will leave this awful place and be my wife! What may I call you, darling?" the prince announced importantly.

But this is not a fairy tale so the damsel did not blush, fall into the handsome prince's strong arms so that she could be carried away to live happily ever after. Instead, what did happen was a loud slap as the woman sat up and smacked the prince across his face.

"You may call me Senteria and that is for kissing me," she explained.

The prince was shocked.

She slapped him again. "That is for insulting my charming little home," she said and slapped him once more. "And that is for presuming I will go with you."

The poor prince recoiled in shock. His cheek had turned a bright shade of scarlet.

"But dear lady, I don't understand. This is what happens. A dashing prince fights through danger, up a dark tower to save the desperate lady who has been trapped!"

The prince calmed himself, deciding that the blow to the dmsel's head had obviously made her delusional. "You are forgiven for your outburst," he said, generously. "Now come with me."

He held his hand down to her but to his amazement she pulled hers away roughly.

"Get out! Get out now or I will set Drafear on you!" she threatened.

The prince was now cold, tired and quickly becoming irritated.

"And who would Drafear be? Your kitten?" He mocked wearily.

"No, my dragon!" Senteria claimed proudly.

The prince laughed, "This is not a fairy tale; there's no such thing!"

He turned to leave. This woman was obviously not one who deserved to marry him. It would just bring shame to his country. His father would be furious if he brought her back to their palace. He wondered what people would think if he returned alone but decided he would explain that the damsel was dangerously unwell so he had left her locked up.

He turned back to Senteria, "A tower is the right place for you. You will be stuck in this fairy tale of a life forever and alone!"

Senteria laughed coldly, "I am in a fairy tale? You are the one who came searching in a dark tower for a future wife."

The prince turned back angrily and to his disgust, saw the damsel making strange signs with her hands and saying words he did not understand. He reconsidered his decision. This woman was obviously a danger to herself and others; he would force her back to the palace and have her locked up in a cell.

"You *will* come back with me. You are obviously unwell and a danger to everyone so you will be locked up in a cell," the prince declared. He reached out towards the woman who was no longer a picture of beauty but of anger. Her face was lined with frown marks and her lips were thin and tight. Her eyes flashed dangerously as she granted him one last chance, "Leave my home now!"

Ignoring her, the prince grabbed her arm, tight enough that she could not escape but not too tight that he would hurt her. Senteria struggled violently to escape from his grasp and shouted,

"Drafear, come to me!" just as she performed her final hand signs.

Two huge horns, followed by a scaly, green head, appeared coming through the broken window. Dark orange eyes, each with a thin black slit for its pupil glared at the prince and dark grey smoke billowed from a large snout. All that could be seen of its body was a thick, green neck.. It opened its mouth, showing off a set of sharp, dangerous teeth, and let out a mighty roar that chilled the prince to his bones. The prince stepped backwards quickly and stumbled to the floor.

# Not A Fairy Tale

"No, no this can't be! Dragons only exist in fairy tales. It's a trick, an illusion, it's magic – you're a witch!" he whimpered.

Senteria laughed, "Magic and witches only exist in fairy tales. Drafear, attack!"

The terrifying dragon opened his mouth wide and out came a scorching ball of fire. The prince threw himself out of the fireball's way and, when it had passed, dived for the door.

Heart pounding he ran back up the corridor and through the door leading out onto the bridge. This time he had no chance to be scared as he could hear heavy footsteps approaching. He shrieked as the dragon brought its huge tail down on the bridge, destroying the part that the prince had just left. The tail moved closer and closer to the prince, breaking the bridge as it went. Fearing for his life the prince dived through door and started sprinting down the spiral staircase three steps at a time. Within a quarter of the time that the stairs had originally taken him, he was at the bottom and racing towards the main door.

He hesitated temporarily before charging through the door to find his trustworthy stallion. Not seeing his stead, he panicked, wondering if it would have been scared away. At that exact moment, he heard the beat of hooves against the hard stone path charging for the exit but then to his delight his beautiful horse caught sight of her rider and galloped into view. Fate had been kind to him and at least made his horse abandon him in the right direction.

"Whoa, calm down," he shouted. "Apone, calm down." Apone, the horse, was terrified but if there was one thing that the prince *was* good at it was looking after horses. He was gentle and loving and Apone adored him. Despite her terror, she stopped for just enough time to let him climb onto her back before racing off once more.

The prince looked back over his shoulder to see Drafear now airborne, its wings spread wide and flying straight for them. He closed his eyes tight and waited for the impact.

Two minutes later, he opened first one eye then the other and looked back. Drafear was back at the tower being stroked by a now calm Senteria.

He was greeted on arrival by the king.

"Ah son you have returned," the King exclaimed. But where is your wife?"

The prince took a deep breath and told his story; as a result, naturally, he was confined to his bed for several weeks as the king declared him ill.

When he finally came out and after much reassurance to his father that he knew dragons did not exist, he decided to visit Apone and go for a ride.

Before long, he saw another rider in the distance and increased his pace to see if he knew them but the rider saw the approach and sped up, starting a playful race around the huge field before they stopped and collapsed exhausted next to each other.

The prince looked over at his riding companion and immediately fell in love. She had long dark hair and beautiful dark eyes which twinkled with a love for mischief. They talked for a while and the prince learned that she was only a peasant and had no link to royalty at all but was surprised to realise that this did not bother him at all.

"What is your name?" She asked.

Usually the prince would have replied with your highness or sir but this time he replied modestly,

"My name is James, beautiful lady, and I would very much like to meet you again sometime."

The couple met regularly after that. Sometimes they rode and other times they just talked. He told her of his adventure and she believed him. At that moment, he knew he would love her forever.

Eventually they were married and lived happily ever after.

Hey, this was rather like a fairy tale wasn't it?

~o~

I was inspired to write this story by accident rather than design. I had decided I would like to write for children but didn't know what exactly I wanted to write. I remember thinking; it should be light hearted but not exactly a fairy tale and from there 'not a fairy-tale' was born. I like writing for children because I spent hours as a child reading and loved every minute of it. As cliché as it sounds, it transported me to many new and exciting worlds. It was my favourite pastime and I would lie awake way past my bedtime reading Enid

Blyton's books repeatedly. I began with her wishing chair and faraway tree series and then progressed onto her stories set in boarding schools, but by far my favourite stories were the *Famous Five*. Enid Blyton and these books in particular, are the reason I love books and writing so much today. Since then I have discovered many amazing authors but her books will always remain special to me and if someday I can write children stories even half as good as hers, I will be overjoyed.

# MATTHEW WILCOX
## STRINGS

Matthew Wilcox is a nineteen-year-old writer who lives in Willenhall, Wolverhampton. Currently reading Creative and Professional Writing and English at the University of Wolverhampton, he is working on his first novel and aims to publish it in the near future. Besides writing, Matthew uses Photoshop to create photographic manipulations of himself in surreal settings, attends weekly karate lessons, and enjoys hill and mountain walking. He also takes great interests in history, philosophy, religion, politics and cartography.

Welcome to Ted Darrow's Primary School.
Shadowy vistas stretch from the school gates to the front doors. It's 2015. January. Thursday. Twenty-seven past eight. Einar and the sister emerge out of the car, bags on their backs. The mother smiles and waves through the window and sets off down the road. Einar and the sister watch. The mother makes a sharp turn left.
Gone.
Einar and the sister walk through the gate. Into the playground. They're just in time: the teachers pour out the front doors in an orderly fashion, in a line, hands behind their backs, and the children race up to them, forming lines of their own before them. Einar and the sister head to their lines.

One of the teachers steps forward and addresses the children: T-shirts tucked in and the top button done up, shoe laces tied properly – and if not shoe laces, the Velcro strapped "perfectly" – stand up straight. And not a word.

Starting from the left to the right—one by one—a teacher and a line of students march towards the front doors and inside. No one else moves until the last child enters the building. Eventually, the sister's teacher and line head in. Then Einar's.

Einar reaches his class. He hangs his coat up. And his bag. Registration passes quickly. Mathematics flies by – Einar likes Maths – so does his father – English is boring. Break time arrives and disappears. Science: they watch a video on a small screen. No one writes a word down.

Religious studies. Einar eyes the clock. The longer hand is in between the eight and nine. The shorter hand is between twelve and one. Dinner time is close. Einar's stomach rumbles. There's already the smell of meat downstairs—the thought of meat spurs another thought—the thought of dessert, chocolate cake with sprinkles—probably even better, chocolate-filled donuts—oh, he can only hope, they're uncommon.

"And remember," says the teacher at the front. He writes on the chalkboard. "God… gave us *all*… Free Will."

Einar eyes the teacher. And notices something.

Strings. Coming from the ceiling. Coming from the hole in the ceiling. The strings dig into the back of the teacher's hand, in the centre. Einar notices several more strings around the teacher's fingers. The strings don't dangle; they aren't limp; they're straight. They pull—control—the teacher's hand.

As the teacher drops his chalk and strolls toward his desk, a "thing," a thing only Einar can describe as "Little Man," appears from the ceiling. This Little Man, as Einar focuses on him, has a comically out-of-proportioned head. Now, this makes Einar smile, up until he can see the Little Man's teeth: barbed. Same with his nose. Two eyes. No ears. Bald. Wings on his back. Einar thinks of butterfly wings. Just without the colours or patterns.

Einar spots another Little Man—two Little Men—several Little Men fly out of the hole in the ceiling. They attach strings to the children's hands and feet and head and chest and bodily joints: elbows, knees, ankles, wrists. Some children have two Little Men with them. The second Little Man puts its hands over the child's head. Each pull a random face. That's it.

Einar looks around, mouth agape. The Little Men ignore him.

"Einar," the teacher shouts. Einar looks back. He sees a second Little Man by the teacher. He holds out a piece of paper in front of his eyes. "Have you written what I told you down?" The Little Man throws the piece of paper away and holds up another. "Come on, write it down, *little boy*."

Einar says nothing. He writes it down: 'God gave us Free Will.'

Dinner time strikes.

The Little Men continue to baffle—amaze—Einar. He wonders why there're no Little Men with strings on him, or hover over him, or even acknowledge him for that matter. It's not just the strings that fascinate Einar, either, it's the pieces of paper, too, like with his religious teacher: these Little Men hold up pieces of paper – that come out of nowhere, at least to Einar's knowledge – in front of the children's and teacher's faces, and on them are a string of words, and the children and teachers read them out. Einar notices one of the Little Men stick a piece of paper into one of the teacher's ear and he starts humming.

Einar takes a tray and stands in the dinner line. He watches the Little Men control the dinner ladies – every movement, to the contraction of the fingers. Above each dinner lady is another Little Man: they hold one of their hands above the dinner ladies' heads – the other hand strokes a finger down their face: indicating feigned crying.

A full tray of food later, Einar sits. Normally, Einar takes five minutes to eat his dinner. Today it takes him thirty minutes. The Little Men distract him as they prance and dance about the dinner hall, the children and teachers and dinner ladies blindly following. He doesn't eat all his food. Not today. It goes cold. Einar hates cold food that's supposed to be hot.

Einar spends the last few moments of dinner time outside, sitting alone against a wall, watching the Little Men control the children and teachers. Other days, he would play pretend guns with his friends or football or stuck in the mud.

Sports is last. Cricket. Einar, though he doesn't like the position, and on most occasions has protested against it, volunteers to be a fielder. He wants to watch all the Little Men. About half way through the game, several of the Little Men come together, along with two kids. Shortly after, the two kids fight: they punch and kick and slap and knee and elbow one another. The Little Men hold the teacher back for a few seconds. Then spur him into action. After a few bruises and a bloody nose, the teacher splits them up.

The Little Men parade about the kids. To Einar, they appear to be laughing.

After cricket, the school day ends.

Einar leaves the school and finds the mother in the car. Several Little Men sprawl about the chassis, by the wheels, on the windshields, the doors, the bonnet. It's not just his car, either. It's everyone else's. About seven, eight, nine of them cover the car, conversing with each other, their tongues flapping about.

Einar opens the door. The back door. His sister has beaten him to the front seat – again. Little Men surround them, both of them. One of the Little Men turns the mother around. Another Little Man wields four metal spikes and prods two at either side of her mouth, lifts it up, causing her to smile. The other two prod her eyebrows, lift them up, causing her eyebrows to arch. A third Little Man holds a piece of paper up, reading 'How was school?'

"How was school?" the mother asks.

"Where did you get those Little Men from?" Einar asks enthusiastically. "Everyone has them in school now!"

The Little Men around the mother burst into activity, jumping up and down, their ant-thorax-like eyebrows knitting together, bearing their barbed teeth at little Einar. After a short conversation, the Little Men start propping up the mother for a response. Two metal spikes prime at her eyebrows, pulling down, causing them to knit together. A Little Man floats over the mother's head, hands over, a face full of rage. The mother replicates it. A piece of paper comes before her: 'I ask you a *s...*'

"I ask you a s-s-s-s-s—" stutters the mother. The Little Man promptly replaces the piece of paper. "Simple question, Einar. And you come out with complete, utter nonsense. Christ. Why are you so…" the piece of paper vanishes. The mother doesn't complete her sentence.

And she says nothing for the rest of the journey home. Einar just watches the Little Men control the car.

He wants his own Little Man.

The sound of gravel reaches Einar's ears. They're home. Professionally, and like chauffeurs, the Little Men open the doors and guide the sister and the mother inside the house. Einar follows. One of the Little Men yanks the sister's arm, closing the door on Einar. Slam. Tap. Tap. Tap. Metal clanks. The mother opens the door; and the Little Men laugh at Einar, pointing, and making – what Einar considers it to be – rude gestures: a flick of the hands, dangling tongues, eyes wide and head spinning as if a cartoon character has been hit on the head by a wooden mallet.

Einar marches to his room, feet stamping, cheeks red, a growl in his throat. He lobs his bag across the room, kicks off his shoes, rips off his school jumper— the mother is at the door, equally as red. The Little Men dance around her, constructing her emotions, preparing her lines, painting her face—

"What are you doing? Just because your sister slammed—"

"Those Little Men did it, they slammed the door in my face, not, not, not my sister," he pants, water in his eyes. "They're around you now—one has a paper in front of you."

The Little Men glare at tiny Einar. They converse briefly, chit-chatting between themselves. Then they haul the mother back. Force her hand to the door. Slams it.

Einar goes on his Playstation 2. To kill time. He succeeds. It calms him down, too.

Soon enough, he smells dinner. The smell brings him to his feet. He rushes downstairs to see a fresh batch of homemade chips, yellow with strips of brown and black, and smiley faces, a few with holes in and slightly brown. The mother opens a cupboard. Half-empty condiments fall out: red sauce, barbeque sauce, mustard. Boxes of out-of-date cereal, torn, damp and crumpled up in the corner, hide underneath chipped bowls.

Einar watches as the mother—the Little Men—prepares the dishes. Chips. Then smiley faces. She snatches the red sauce. Squirts it on. Slides the dish across the counter to Einar. She utters not a word. He collects his knife and fork and heads into the living room.

Sits. Finds his groove in the settee. Starts eating. He watches the cartoons. There're no Little Men inside controlling the characters. But he imagines them being there, controlling their arms with strings, their faces with metal spikes, and putting pieces of paper in front of them.

He hears the door bang. A voice booms throughout the house, "I'm home." It's the father with his signature greeting. Einar turns to the door to see a shadow, several shadows, drawing longer on the door. The father's head appears around the door. A grin on his face, with the help of the Little Men and the metal spikes. Intimidation centres on Einar.

"You got them, too?" Einar asks. "The Little Men."

The Little Men repaint the father. They make his fist fly over his shoulder, his thumb sticking out, a knitted brow above his forehead, paper in front of him.

"Right, *little boy*. Your mother has told me about this. We need to talk, okay? Hurry up. Eat that. We'll take Laplace for a walk."

Laplace is the family dog. A demon to the neighbours.

Einar agrees to go. He rams down the rest of the chips and smiley faces, puts his walking boots on and waits for the father. Laplace trots through the door into the living room with an aristocratic demeanour—posh—civilised—seemingly intelligent. Several Little Men pull the strings on the dog's paws, head, ears, nose, mouth and swinging tail. Another Little Man, above Laplace, opens and closes his mouth. Open—bark—close. Open—bark-bark—close. Laplace starts bouncing.

The father walks in.

"Okay, alright. Let's go, Laplace. Come on, little boy."

Einar shadows his father out the door. Off the gravel. Along the path. On the field. The father—the Little Men—lets Laplace off the lead. The Little Men run Laplace up the field, through the tree line. Einar draws up to the father's side. The Little Men make room for him. There's silence between the father and Einar.

As they draw closer to the tree line, the father turns to the son. The Little Men prep the father.

"Okay, Einar. These so-called Little Men you keep seeing, they're just your imaginary friends. Okay? They don't exist."

"But they do, Dad. They're flying around you now. Don't you see the strings in your hands?"

"I have no strings in my hands. Look. None. See? These Little Men – they don't—"

Barks sound off in the distance. It's Laplace. The son and father, in unison, run. Run towards Laplace. He is still barking. They find him with another dog and its owner. The Little Men orchestrate the entire scenario: Laplace and the other dog scrap, mouths wide, aiming for the neck, on hind legs, almost as if they're trying to eat one another. The Little Men hold the owners back, but at the same time make them lean forward as if ready to split the dogs up.

Einar cracks.

"Stop it!" He shouts. "Stop making them fight, Little Men. Just stop. I have had enough of you controlling everyone—"

Click. Show time.

I hover down. A few of my fellow "Little Men" behind me. We're quick to assemble ourselves around Einar. I commandeer his movements – the arms and hands and fingers, everything – while everyone else commands his thoughts, his speech and his emotions. We're ready. I nod at the other Little Men. They acknowledge the signal. They stop the fighting. Then I motion to the one who controls the brain. He waves his hand in front of the boy's eyes.

"They don't exist," says the father.

I make Einar look around frantically; looking at the father's hands; looking at the dogs' paws, the tails. The controller of emotions sends a wave of confusion, and then relief. Einar breathes out. I move his hands over his head. Then by his side.

"Oi. Naughty boy," says the other dog owner, wagging his finger. "Sorry about that. He started it."

We laugh. No he didn't. Ha-ha.

"No, no, don't worry about it," says the father. One of the Little Men raises a finger. "No treats for you when we get back Mr. Laplace. See ya."

We walk them off in separate directions.

Together, we make Einar come to the realisation we don't exist. Paper. Emotions. Movement. Thought.

"Dad… they're all gone." Einar says.

"They never existed in the first place, Einar. They were just your imaginary friends."

"Oh…"

"Come on, forget about it now."

And we make sure he does.

~o~

Matthew Wilcox

The main source of inspiration for this short story came to me when I was watching a video of Christopher Hitchens discussing religion with Tony Jones. Part way through his discourse, he weaves in the topic of Free Will, saying: "when the question is put 'is there Free Will?' the believer will say 'yes because we've been given it. Of course there's Free Will, the Big Guy says so.'" He later adds, rather comically, "my answer when I'm asked 'is there Free Will?' I say, 'yeah, there is Free Will, we have Free Will, we have no choice.'"

The moment I heard this, it stuck with me, and still sticks to me. It was beautiful, a beautiful example of philosophical irony. So beautiful in fact, it's the central theme, the heart, of the short story.

And this is what I love about writing: I can express a message creatively. I can convey the irony of having no choice but to have Free Will as someone saying they have Free Will but really has no control over their actions at all, and instead some Little Men do their actions for them. That, to me, is fantastic – and liberating, too. Ultimately, when I set out to write, this is what I aim to do: convey a message or theme.

# HARRIET AVERY
## ISLA

Harriet Avery is a twenty-two-year-old writer of prose who hails from the windy coastal town of Felixstowe in Suffolk. She recently completed her undergraduate degree on the fabled creative writing course at the University of East Anglia, and is looking forward to returning for her Masters in Prose. As well as being selected for the annual Undergraduate anthologies whilst at university, she has also been published in *The Red Line* and *Henshaw Press*, amongst others. She enjoys reading her work live at spoken word events.

*Monday*

This morning, my wife decided to have an existential crisis.

I didn't realise straightaway. In my defence, I was running late. The alarm clock had, for reasons presumably best known to itself, decided not to go off, so when I finally opened my eyes, expecting to see seven o'clock, there it was, with five to eight grinning smugly all over its face.

Cue twenty minutes of panicked running around in my pyjama bottoms trying to clean my teeth and drink coffee at the same time. I must have glanced at Sian at least twice – she was still in bed of course – and noticed nothing out of the ordinary. Same face, same hair, same nightie, same everything.

She got up as I was getting dressed, and wandered downstairs – I couldn't find that tie I really wanted, the one with the gold pattern, sort of swirls and dots. I like it. Sian bought it for me a long time ago. It looks a good deal more expensive than it actually was – so even if I haven't quite got it together, at least that tie makes it look as if I have. Draws the eye, you know.

I shouted down to Sian: 'Sian? Do you know where my tie is?'

No answer. 'You know the one! With the... with the... with..." I gestured expansively, expecting her to be in the doorway already, like she always is, waiting with the usual tired expression on her face. But, as I turned, she wasn't there.

Thundering downstairs, I found Sian standing in the kitchen. She looked at me with surprise.

'Oh sorry,' she said. 'I didn't realise you were talking to me. I'm afraid I'm not Sian today.'

I stared at her, and sighed impatiently. 'What?'

'I don't feel like I'm Sian anymore.' Her eyes wandered past me, examining her favourite Jack Vettriano calendar on the wall.

'OK.' I pinched the bridge of my nose and breathed deeply. 'Could you possibly pick a slightly less stressful time to have an existential crisis, and tell me where my gold tie is instead?'

She reached for me as if she were going to produce the tie from behind my ear – and then proceeded to pull the calendar off the wall. 'Sorry – I'm slightly distracted – that picture is *incredibly* ugly.'

Sian loves Vettriano. Our house is covered in prints of women in fancy clothes dancing on beaches and smoking in diners and sitting in cars. But now, she was flicking through the pages with an expression of distaste. 'Wow. So... two-dimensional. How could Sian like this stuff?'

'Why are you referring to yourself in the third person?' I said. 'It's really annoying.'

'Sorry, Mark, but Sian isn't me,' she said. 'Today, I think you should start calling me... Isla.'

*Tuesday*

I came home from work to find the house smelling overpoweringly of Eastern spices. There were incense candles burning in the lounge. One of them had set fire to a dream-catcher hanging in the window. I stared at it for a second; and then left it burning, and went to find Sian.

I found her in the kitchen, her usual place when I came home from the office. Then I realised she was making sushi.

'Sian, we don't like sushi,' I said.

'Actually,' she said. '*I* do.'

I sighed. This midlife-crisis-thing was getting out of control. 'Sian, I wish you'd stop this. I told you about the incense yesterday – and I've had a long day – and those candles are a fire hazard –'

'Sian didn't like them either, did she? That's right, I remember...' She finished wrapping that dark green stuff around the rice and fish, and then I watched as she popped them in her mouth one by one, wiping the corners of her lips with quick dabs of her fingertips. It was a most un-Sian-like gesture.

'Now, I'm going out.' She tossed the knife at the sink. It landed in the breadbin.

'You're going out?' This stopped me in my tracks. 'But what will I have for dinner? Have you left something in the fridge?'

'No, sorry – I suppose you'll have to cook something for yourself.' She was pulling on her coat. 'I'm sorry, Mark, but I'm not your wife.'

'What do you mean, you're not my wife?'

'Check your wedding certificate. Don't think you'll find *Isla* written anywhere.'

'But it's film night tonight – it's your week to choose...'

The front door closed. She was gone.

*Wednesday*

In the end, I managed to convince her to come with me to see a psychiatrist today. He had bushy eyebrows, and was reassuringly Austrian.

I took a moment to check he was good and aware that he was being paid to sort out Sian's little delusion, and then waited reluctantly outside as he asked her some questions. When I came in again, Sian was looking irritated. It was a comfortingly familiar expression.

'So. I have managed to deduce that the lady has no specific history of trauma –' the psychiatrist began, and was promptly interrupted. .

'As I keep telling you, it's *Sian* who has no history of trauma,' Sian said. 'Not "*the lady*", not *this* lady. Sian. Not me, not anymore.'

The psychiatrist smiled thinly. 'Indeed,' he said, with devastating patience, and then turned back to me. 'Of course, it is perfectly possible that the subconscious mind is blocking the trauma out,' he explained. 'In fact, anything negative might be blocked. So, really, we cannot take anything she says to be the truth.'

'What a useful perspective to have when interviewing patients,' Sian muttered, digging her nails into the arm-rest.

In the end, he wrote her a diagnosis of Dissociative Personality Disorder, and prescribed her a course of sedative drugs.

*Thursday*

Sian wrote a list today. Apparently, it's to help me "separate the past and the present":

*Sian likes cornflakes. Isla likes yoghurt and fruit.*
*Sian likes driving to the shops. Isla prefers walking whenever possible.*
*Sian likes green grapes. Isla likes black grapes.*
*Sian hates leaving the television on when we're not watching. Isla hates silence.*
*Sian works part-time in the local library. Isla refuses to work for such a bureaucratic, pedestrian establishment.*

She pinned it on the fridge with a magnet, with another page underneath so she can keep adding things when she thinks of them. She also refused to take the drugs prescribed by Dr Kaufmann. She maintains that it's because she's not ill.

'Mentally ill people often don't know they're mentally ill,' I said.

'Then how do you know that you're not?' she pointed out.

I didn't have an answer.

*Friday*

This morning, I came up with an answer.

'Because I'm acting perfectly rationally!' I told her, as she sorted through the wardrobe, tossing all of her favourite clothes into a bin-bag which she'd labelled "*FOR OXFAM*". I noticed her handwriting had changed.

'As am I,' she returned.

I snatched up the bag, and rustled it in her face. '*This* is rational?'

She sighed impatiently. 'I'm throwing away outfits I don't like. What's irrational about that? In fact, some would argue that it's more rational than holding onto things that haven't been worn since – what, 1990?'

She was disentangling one of my shirts from the wardrobe depths much as a surgeon might pull a tapeworm out of an intestinal tract. It was one of my more garish Hawaiian ones.

'I bought that in Ibiza,' I said – and then it hit me. 'Wait – that holiday *was* in 1990! The year before we got married! You and me, Sian – you knew that! You remember it!'

'Certainly I remember it,' she replied, still rummaging through the clothes. 'But not as something that happened to *me*. Why would I choose to go to such a nasty touristy place? Oh boy, I hope you never wore this with that shirt!'

She emerged from the wardrobe with an expression of amusement. Dangling from her finger was my blue-and-gold tie.

*Saturday*

Having moved the TV into the kitchen, (in an effort to humour Sian's newly developed passion for cooking along with the TV chefs) I found her, at lunchtime, leaning against the oven, watching some programme about Paris. She ignored me entirely. Together, we watched a panning shot down the Champs Elysees. The sun was shining. There were fashionable French people strolling down the pavements. The traffic was juddering around the Arc de Triomph.

Next to me, Sian sighed longingly. '*C'est magnifique, non?*' She put both hands out towards the screen as if she could take hold of the images and pull them to her. 'Do you remember? On our honeymoon – all those little patisseries, and the cafes on the corners – and *La Tour Eiffel.*'

I rolled my eyes. 'No – if you recall, we honeymooned in Mexico,' I said. 'We've never been to Paris.'

Her response was worrying. 'Don't be dense, John,' she said. 'It wasn't that long ago.'

'Who's John?' I said.

She looked at me, bemused. Then her face changed, and I saw she was as freaked out as I was, for the first time.

'I… don't know,' she said. The oven suddenly beeped, like a confirmation buzzer on a game-show.

We stared at each other. The oven continued to peep insistently.

'Sian...' I began, but stopped, as she turned to pull on oven gloves and open the door. She was instantly enveloped in a cloud of steam. I waited until she emerged, holding a fresh-baked quiche.

She closed the oven door with a bang.

'Sian...' I said again. But she tore the oven gloves off, threw them down, and glared at me.

'Oh, just forget it, Mark,' she said, and then, as I stood, not knowing what to say, she strode out of the room.

The quiche remained in the kitchen until it was stone-cold.

*Sunday*

This morning, Sian announced that she had booked herself a session with a psychologist.

This took me by surprise. 'I thought you said that you weren't ill?'

She looked disgruntled. 'I'm not. But I'm not so blind as to think that the current situation is *normal*.'

'So we're going back to Dr Kaufmann?'

'No. I've booked up someone else.'

The name of this new psychologist is Dr Eamont. I looked him up on Google. Apparently, he specialised in hypnotherapy.

*Monday*

So there I was, for the second time in a week, in a waiting room outside a psychiatric office, wondering why all the posters warning against suicide are quite so depressing, while Sian was interviewed within. It seemed to take an extraordinarily long time.

As it turns out, I am not a fan of psychiatrist's waiting rooms. Your imagination can run riot about the other people in there with you – who's the most psychopathic? Who is the most depressed? Who's murdered their girlfriend and buried her body in the woods? When the girl on reception informed me that I could at last go back in, I even caught myself wondering whether she might actually be a perfectly ordinary woman who was simply suffering from the delusion that she was a receptionist.

I closed the door behind me. Sian was sitting on one chair. He was sitting on the other. The only other option was the leather recliner chair. I opted to stand.

He explained to me that Sian was a very interesting case. He told me that, with no history of trauma, there was no reason to suspect Dissociative Personality Disorder, or Transient Global Amnesia or anything like that. 'In fact,' he said, 'it is Isla who seems to be having problems with amnesia.'

'Isla isn't real,' I reminded him patiently. 'Isla is Sian's delusion.'

He looked delighted. 'Well,' he said. 'Actually, as I put your wife under hypnosis, I was finding that there was no disassociation between different histories; there was no clash of personalities; no awareness of time loss or identity confusion. What I mean is: your wife knew of Sian, as one would know of a friend – or really, a friend of a friend. She could not communicate *as* Sian. Which, in turn, means that your wife's subconscious mind, *as well as* her conscious mind, entirely believes itself to be someone *other than your wife*. She has, in effect, changed identity.'

He seemed to be expecting me to leap up and punch the air, or perhaps feel a sudden weakness at the knees, and need to sit down quickly. I did neither of these things.

Instead I said 'Well, hang on.' I thought the good doctor was just running away with his ridiculous theories – I said as much. 'You can't just switch from one person to another. It's ridiculous. You said she "believes" herself to be someone else. Well, that's not the same as *being* someone else, is it? Surely, it's just a sort of delusion.' I ended hopefully.

'Oh, I think it's rather more than that,' he replied, steepling his fingers and resting his chin on the very tips. 'You have to ask yourself, Mr Greenbeck: if our identity is not the person whom we *believe* ourselves to be, then what exactly is it?'

I found him extremely tiresome. I said so to Sian, as she drove back. (I couldn't be bothered to tell her that she had never learnt to drive.) Then, as we reached the town centre, she suddenly pulled over, and insisted on buying me a coffee in Costa. She said I looked "rattled".

Inside, the hot chocolate machine was playing up, and, typically, the couple in front of us insisted on ordering hot chocolate, so we had to wait forever. Sian then decided to order hot chocolate as well. I mused miserably about how the old Sian used to detest hot chocolate.

As we sat down, I was feeling decidedly gloomy. Eamont's final irritating words of wisdom were ringing in my ears: '*If you want my advice,*' he'd said, as he ushered us through his door. *'I think you need to accept that Isla is here now, and set about finding Sian.'* Sian herself seemed surprisingly perky, dunking the marshmallows with her spoon until they melted into a pink-and-white gooey mess. I couldn't understand it. 'Aren't you a little bit upset to learn that you have somehow lost yourself? You might never find your proper, real identity again.'

She just shrugged. 'I was brought up as an optimist,' she said. '*Que sera sera,* you know?' She sucked on her spoon philosophically for a moment, and then stood up. 'And now I'm going to get more marshmallows.'

Left alone, I found myself with nothing to do except listen to the other couple, the ones who'd ordered the hot chocolates. The man was whining. 'I'm just saying, you're going to give yourself a nervous breakdown.'

'Hilarious,' I heard the woman with him sigh sarcastically.

What could possibly be happening in their lives which is so bad? I wondered bitterly. They were huddled over their cups, not looking at each other.

As I glanced round at them, the woman stood up, long blonde hair swinging. She said something like: 'sorry – look, John, would you mind if I change to coffee? I actually detest hot chocolate.'

At that moment, she saw Sian across the café. Her expression changed to a frown. She walked towards Sian.

Stirring marshmallows into her drink, Sian almost didn't notice as the woman came to a halt in front of her. Then she stopped. Her eyes took in the stranger in front of her. There was a long moment of silence as they seemed to study each other. I found that both I, and the man at the other table, had stood up.

Then, the woman put out her hand, and smiled. 'So you're Isla,' said the woman. 'Hello. I'm Sian.'

~o~

Stories are built on character. Take the Virginia Woolf novel, *Mrs Dalloway*. During the novel, in actuality, very little happens. A woman goes out to buy flowers. A plane flies over London. A man and a woman trim a hat. But the novel still manages to be compelling. The reason that we read on is because we want find out about the hidden lives and secrets which make up the Warren Smiths, and Mrs Dalloway herself.

In essence, the same could be said throughout literature – we are fascinated by the interaction between Gaskell's Margaret Hale and the seemingly implacable Mr Thornton; how Kathy and Tommy and Ruth cope with Ishiguro's dystopian world; even how it turns out for that misguided pair, the Macbeths. Our interest comes from the people.

As a writer, I am intrigued by how words on a page can create what seems to be a real flesh-and-blood person. For the short piece, *Isla*, I wanted to play with the idea that identity in a fictional world is not necessarily a stable thing. Rather than place this in a dramatic, sci-fi setting, I was more interested in how it might play out in the distinctly average lives of a typical, middle-class, suburban couple. Think *Talking Heads*, rather than *Titus Andronicus*. How, in their little grey slice of reality, would Mr and Mrs Greenbeck cope with what they can only understand as the onset of a rather strong mid-life crisis?

Of course, *Isla* is nothing like any of the works mentioned above. But then, if it was, perhaps it wouldn't be worth reading.

Printed in Great Britain
by Amazon.co.uk, Ltd.,
Marston Gate.